DALLAS LOVETT'S
WOVEN BEAD & WIRE JEWELRY

DALLAS LOVETT'S
WOVEN BEAD & WIRE JEWELRY

25 GORGEOUS PROJECTS

LARK

LARK JEWELRY & BEADING

An Imprint of Sterling Publishing
387 Park Avenue South
New York, NY 10016

ISBN 978-1-4547-0807-0

Library of Congress Cataloging-in-Publication Data
Lovett, Dallas.
Dallas Lovett's woven bead & wire jewelry : 25 gorgeous projects.
    pages cm
Includes index.
ISBN 978-1-4547-0807-0 (pbk.)
1. Jewelry making. 2. Wire craft. 3. Beadwork. 4. Beads. I. Title. II. Title: Woven bead
    and wire jewelry.
TT212.L685 2014
745.594'2—dc23
                    2013032954

Distributed in Canada by Sterling Publishing
c/o Canadian Manda Group, 165 Dufferin Street
Toronto, Ontario, Canada M6K 3H6
Distributed in the United Kingdom by GMC Distribution Services
Castle Place, 166 High Street, Lewes, East Sussex, England BN7 1XU
Distributed in Australia by Capricorn Link (Australia) Pty. Ltd.
P.O. Box 704, Windsor, NSW 2756, Australia

For information about custom editions, special sales, and premium and corporate purchases, please
contact Sterling Special Sales at 800-805-5489 or specialsales@sterlingpublishing.com.

Email academic@larkbooks.com for information about desk and examination copies.
The complete policy can be found at larkcrafts.com.

Every effort has been made to ensure that all the information in this book is accurate. However, due to
differing conditions, tools, and individual skills, the publisher cannot be responsible for any injuries,
losses, and other damages that may result from the use of the information in this book.

Manufactured in China

2 4 6 8 10 9 7 5 3 1

larkcrafts.com

CONTENTS

INTRODUCTION 8

SUPPLIES 9
Materials 9
Tools 11

TECHNIQUES 14
Basic Wire Techniques 14
Wire Weaving Techniques 17
Making Findings 23
Torch Techniques 25

RINGS FOR EARS & FINGERS 27
High Rise Earrings 28
Crystal Magic Earrings 30
Quasar Earrings 32
The Ring 35
La Fiesta Earrings 38

BRACELETS & CUFFS 41
Carré Bracelet................................ 42
Braids Bracelet 46
Infinity Bracelet 49
Arthurian Cuff 52
Rain Forest Bracelet 56
Enchanted Bracelet........................... 60
Circles Bracelet 64

PENDANTS 69
Entrapped Elegance Pendant 70
Saturn Pendant 72
Crown Jewel Pendant 76
Forbidden Fruit Pendant 78
De Ros Pendant 81
Phoenix Rising Pendant 84

NECKLACES 89
Interchangeable Necklace 90
Nefertiti Necklace 92
Moroccan Jewels Necklace 96
Diamonds Necklace 99
Wire-Go-Round Necklace 102
Dreamscape Necklace 106
Cleopatra Necklace 110

GALLERY 114

ABOUT THE AUTHOR 118

ACKNOWLEDGMENTS 118

INDEX 119

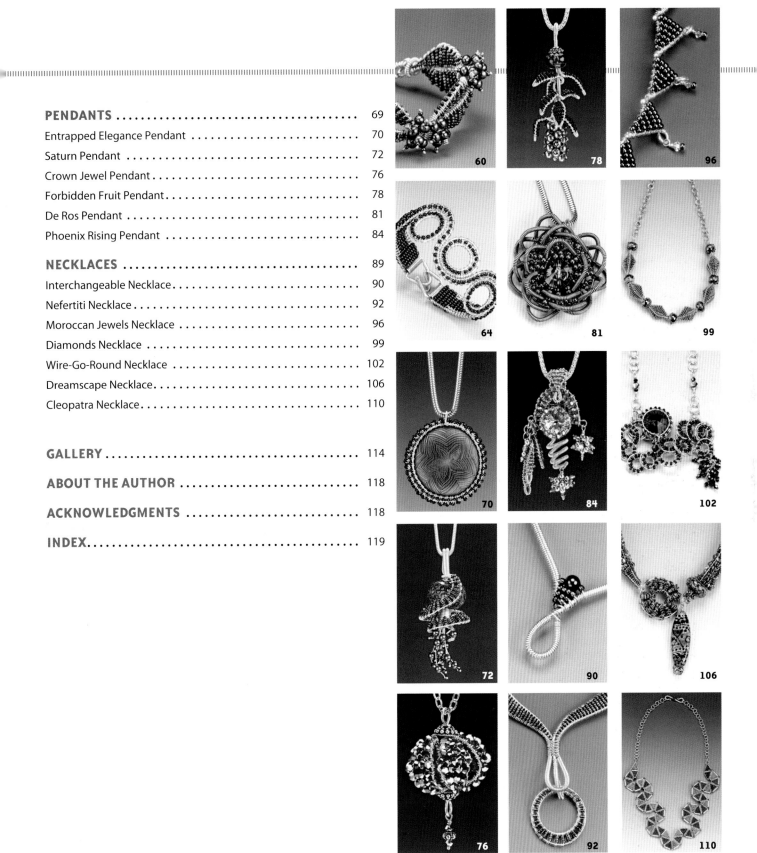

INTRODUCTION

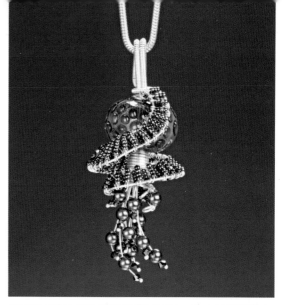

Wire art in some form has been used by many civilizations throughout history, and wire wrapping is one of the oldest methods of making handmade jewelry. Artifacts have been found from as far back as the ancient Phoenicians and in Egyptian tombs 4,000 years old. It's believed that an Egyptian goldsmith produced the first piece of jewelry made entirely of wire. Designs and techniques have been passed down through the ages and wire artists today practice these same techniques in their work.

This book is one of the first to present instructions for making jewelry that combines seed beads with wire and wire weaving. In these pages, I begin by introducing you to the supplies I use. I then take you through the basics of wire weaving, which is the foundation of all the projects. My three main techniques are flat, dimensional, and bezel weaving. In the 25 projects that follow, the instructions take something that looks complicated and breaks it down into a simple step-by-step process, giving you guidance the entire way.

I used flat weaving to make the Saturn Pendant (page 72). In this piece, the weaving is sculpted around a large focal bead. The engineering challenge was how to securely attach the many wires of the "spray" into the main body of the piece.

The Dreamscape Necklace (page 106) is an example of dimensional weaving. Parallel core wires form the armature of a tube, around which you weave. To enlarge the tube, you simply increase the bead count. In this piece, keishi pearls and Bali silver beads create a lot of texture, which is a key feature of the design.

In bezel weaving, you build a basket of wire and beads that holds and enhances a cabochon, as shown in the Entrapped Elegance Pendant (page 70). In this process, a core wire moves in a continuous circle as it embraces the cabochon.

My hope is that as you practice and develop your wire techniques while making my designs, you'll begin to discover your own style and path. Weave it, wire it, Lovett.

Dallas Lovett

SUPPLIES

Materials

Always buy the best quality materials you can afford.

The Bead Box

Beads bring wire jewelry to life. They come in different finishes and can be shiny and smooth; matte; metallic or galvanized; and faceted. Beads of varying types add color, shine, and interest to a piece. I use the following beads for the projects in this book, but you can use other beads with similar sizes and shapes if you prefer.

Seed beads are small glass beads. For wirework, sizes 15° and 11° are generally used, and fit well on smaller gauges of wire.

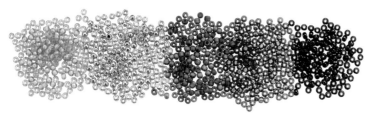

Crystal beads and **gemstone beads** come in a variety of sizes, shapes, colors, and facets. Facets catch light, helping to draw the eye to the jewelry.

A **cabochon** is a convex stone with a flat back. You'll see lots of round or oval cabochons in the projects in this book.

Rivolis are made from lead crystal. They are round, have no holes, and come to a point on the front and back. Many have foiled backs, which provide a reflective surface and vivid color.

Lampworked beads are handmade glass beads created over a flame. They're used as a focal point in jewelry and can help anchor and inspire the design.

Rather than freshwater pearls, **crystal pearls** are used in wirework because they come in a variety of colors and have a larger hole for accommodating wire. They also offer more consistent and precise sizes and shapes. In virtually every project included, you can substitute freshwater pearls of the same size, as long as the bead holes are large enough to accommodate the gauge of wire being used. For example, 20-gauge wire can fit through the holes in 3-mm crystal pearls, but not through the holes in freshwater pearls of the same size.

Keishi pearls are formed when a mollusk shell ejects the original pearl but still continues to make a pearl. For that reason, keishi pearls are available in unusual shapes and a variety of sizes and colors.

Bali silver is sterling silver components like spacers and bead caps that are made on the island of Bali, in Indonesia. Genuine Bali silver is made entirely by hand, starting with the weighing, melting, and mixing of a ratio of 92.5% silver to 7.5% copper.

Wire

The projects in this book are made primarily of sterling silver wire and silver-filled wire. Silver-filled wire has a thick layer of sterling clad over a core of copper or brass. It looks and feels almost the same as sterling silver. Sterling silver wire is composed of 92.5% pure silver and 7.5% copper.

Wire is measured by gauge, which is the term for the diameter of the wire. Small diameters have high numbers, and large diameters are expressed with lower numbers. The jewelry in this book is made in wire from 26-gauge to 16-gauge. Wire also comes in different tempers, or levels of hardness: dead-soft, half-hard, and hard. Most of the projects in the book use dead-soft wire exclusively, because it can be more easily woven, wrapped, and shaped. Half-hard wire works well for making jump rings, ear wires, or findings that require a stiffer structure, but it isn't a good choice for wrapping or weaving.

Wire hardens when it's pulled, shaped, or manipulated; this is known as work hardening. Wire that's kinked or work hardened can become brittle and snap.

Findings

Jump rings come in an infinite range of sizes and gauges. Unless your studio is set up with a special cutter blade and tool, the best option is to find a quality supplier and buy commercially produced rings.

In other books, you might find clasps, chain, ear wires, and head pins mentioned under this heading. You can buy these if you want, but I make my own and I'll teach you how in the Techniques section.

Chemicals

You can buy these at jewelry supply stores.

Self-pickling flux is a liquid compound that keeps wire clean during soldering. It melts onto the surface, and forms a glassy coating, protecting the metal from firescale. You must use the type formulated for soldering silver. For convenience, fill a trigger spray bottle with flux so you can spray it directly onto the metal surface.

Pickle is an acidic solution (sodium bisulfate) that removes firescale and oxidation from silver and copper. Never mix different metals in the same batch of pickle, as it will contaminate the solution. Use a crock pot or a potpourri pot to keep the pickle heated and ready to use, and always remember to turn it off when finished!

Liver of sulfur is a solution that quickly oxidizes or tarnishes metal. It darkens or "antiques" silver and bronze. It comes in a solid, liquid, or paste form. The three factors that affect oxidation are the strength of the solution, its temperature, and the cleanliness of the metal when it's put into the solution.

Solder

Silver solder, available from jewelry supply stores, is an alloy of silver and zinc that's used for joining metal to metal. Although it comes in three types (easy, medium, and hard), for the projects in this book, you will only use easy solder. Solder is available in sheet or wire form. Use sheet solder. It's easier to distinguish when used to solder wire (wire solder looks almost exactly the same as silver wire).

Using solder shears, cut the sheet into small pieces, called pallions, no larger than 1/16 inch (1.6 mm) square. The only soldering technique necessary to complete the projects in this book is the soldering of rings (page 26), and this uses easy solder, which flows at 1355°F (735°C).

Tools

All of the tools used for basic wire work are available from jewelry supply stores, and many can be purchased from your local bead store. It's best to try a tool before you buy it, to ensure that it feels comfortable in your hand and performs as you expect. Wireworking pliers should always have smooth jaws, not serrated ones.

Wireworking Tools

Chain-nose pliers have smooth jaws that taper to a narrow tip. They're used for gripping and bending, holding and stabilizing, making crisp bends, and opening and closing jump rings.

Round-nose pliers have smooth, round jaws and taper to a fine point. Use them for making round loops and bends for eye pins, ear wires, clasps, and jump rings.

Nylon jaw pliers are large, flat pliers with replaceable nylon inserts. Use them to smooth out kinked wire.

Flush cutters are for trimming ends, leaving a square, clean cut. The blades are pointed, with one flat side, and one pinching, angled side. Every cut leaves one flat end and one pointy end. Make sure that the ends of wires are always flush cut, especially when working with heavier gauges of wire, such as 16- or 18-gauge. A flush cut is crucial for wirework, making good cutters an indispensable tool.

Treat flush cutters with care to ensure a long life. Never use them to cut memory wire or any other steel wire, because steel permanently damages the tool.

Chasing hammers have a smooth, convex face and are used to flatten, harden, and reshape wire. **Steel bench blocks** are solid steel and are the smooth, hard surface upon which you'll hammer wire and metal. They can be found in a variety of shapes and sizes.

Rawhide mallets are made of high-grade leather, and are just the thing for hardening and shaping soft wire without marring, scratching, or flattening it.

Awls have a small handle and a straight, fine, tapered point. They're perfect for picking, probing, and pushing apart wires or beads.

Metal files are used to buff out snags and points in wire and metal, and to clean and prepare solder joints. A variety of file sizes, shapes, and grits are available. They come in heavy, half round, triangle, and flat; flat files are most useful for wirework.

Emery boards are an inexpensive, disposable solution for filing out rough marks, ends, or edges.

Tapered steel **ring mandrels** are used to size, shape, and support wire or metal while hammering it into a circular shape. They're also a measuring guide, marked with ring sizes.

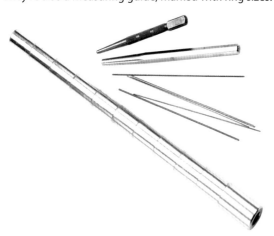

Soldering Tools

Jewelry and lapidary suppliers carry most or all of the tools used for soldering, and some can even be found at your local hardware store.

Micro torches have a fine-point flame and are used to solder joints and make head pins. Use a torch with a temperature range up to 2500° for smaller projects. A micro torch can solder wire as heavy as 16 gauge. Small kitchen torches create enough heat for some applications, but they use fuel less efficiently and tend to overheat. The torches sold by jewelry suppliers are sturdier, produce a hotter flame, and will last for years.

Fire bricks are made from a non-asbestos, fireproof ceramic material that reflects heat back toward its surface, heating the metal more evenly to make soldering fast and efficient. The block is made of fibrous material, so objects can be pinned to the surface and positioned for more precise solder joints. Fire bricks can be purchased from jewelry suppliers and some hardware stores.

Cookie sheets are a perfect, inexpensive work surface for soldering. When working with a flame and hot metal, you must have a flat, fireproof material to protect your work area from damage.

Jewelry tweezers with a fine point are indispensable for positioning small cut pieces of solder in just the right place to help guarantee a clean solder joint. They're sturdier and larger than cosmetic tweezers, and made to handle the heat and stress of jewelry making.

Copper tongs are designed to safely pick up hot metal items and insert them into, or remove them from, a pickling solution. *Don't ever use steel tongs with pickle!* Placing any kind of steel tool into the pickle causes the ions in the copper-rich solution to "jump back" onto the metal that you're trying to clean, effectively copper-plating the metal.

Finishing Tools

Rotary tumblers are small barrel-shaped, rotating machines filled with detergent and steel shot in various shapes and sizes. Drop soldered wire findings and finished jewelry inside, close the lid, leave the machine on for a while, and pull out burnished and polished pieces. **Stainless steel shot** consists of highly polished stainless steel pieces in a mixture of three shapes: diagonal, round, and pin. The variety of shapes helps polish tight spaces and flat areas of jewelry to a bright, mirror finish.

Natural stones, pearls, and soft materials should *not* be tumbled with steel shot, because they will be dulled and damaged. Crystals and glass seed beads can be tumbled with little concern, unless they have galvanized or plated coatings that might scratch or rub off.

Polishing pads are soft square pads with a bonded, micro-abrasive surface. They intensify shine and remove tarnish, discoloration, and oils from metal surfaces.

Additional Tools

A flexible **tape measure** made from soft plastic or fabric will allow you to measure around the wrist or neck for accurate jewelry sizing.

A **drill** allows you to twist any gauge of wire into a tube quickly and easily. It's important that the drill chuck be able to firmly close onto whatever size mandrel you're using.

MANDREL SIZE CHART

Gauge	Decimal inches	Millimeters
12	.08 inch	2.1 mm
14	.06 inch	1.6 mm
16	.05 inch	1.3 mm
18	.04 inch	1 mm
20	.03 inch	0.8 mm

Steel rods, sometimes referred to as **mandrels**, are what you wrap wire around. It's good to have a collection of rods in different sizes. Use the chart above to determine the proper rod size needed.

Wire gauge guides are slotted metal disks that measure the thickness, or gauge, of wire and sheet metal. Thinner wire or metal has high numbers, and thicker wire or metal has low numbers. The wire gauge guide shows the measurements in three different ways: in inches, millimeters, and gauges. The tool has small slots along the side that equal the thickness of the metal. The hole at the end of the slot allows for free movement of the metal, but isn't used for measuring. The correct size of wire or sheet metal fits snugly into the slot.

14-in-1 measuring gauge is a handy little aluminum tool for measuring small-scale work (under 2 inches [5.1 cm]). It has four sides, 14 different measurements from ⅛ to 1½ inches (0.3 to 3.8 cm), and is available in quilting stores.

Rulers are critical tools for making accurate measurements, which is key for successful wirework.

Ultra-fine permanent markers have fade- and water-resistant ink and work well on all metals.

Beading mats can be made of craft foam, leather, or fabric. A good work surface prevents tools, wire, and beads from moving around.

TECHNIQUES

Basic Wire Techniques

Every project in this book uses an array of fundamental skills and techniques. Most techniques in this section are executed with pliers, cutters, and your hands. Production done this way, strictly with hand tools, is known as cold working, and is the basis of all jewelry making.

Straightening Wire

Grasp the wire between the nylon jaw pliers and pull it through. Doing this excessively will harden the wire, making it brittle, so be cautious when using this tool with smaller gauges of wire, such as 24-, 26-, and 28- gauge.

Right-Angle Bend

Use an ultra-fine marker to mark the spot where you want a bend in the wire. Place the chain-nose pliers next to the mark, leaving a distance about equal to the width of the mark. To create a 90° bend, hold the chain-nose pliers in your dominant hand. Use your non-dominant thumb to push the wire firmly against the pliers. When done correctly, the mark will end up in the middle of the bend (figure 1).

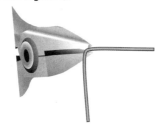

figure 1

Basic Round Loop

Grasp the end of the wire between the round-nose pliers at a point on the jaws that corresponds to the desired diameter of the loop. The end of the wire should not extend past the sides of the jaws. Hold the pliers with the dominant hand; roll the tool toward your body while pushing firmly against the wire in the opposite direction with the other thumb (figure 2). Lack of firm pressure will create a teardrop shape instead of a round loop. After forming the loop, use chain-nose pliers to bend the base and center the loop (figure 3).

figure 2

figure 3

Wrapped Loop

Mark the wire 2 to 2½ inches (5.1–6.4 cm) from the end with a permanent marker. (This leaves a long tail, which is easier to bend.) Grasp the wire where the jaw diameter matches the diameter of the desired loop size and pull the wire around the pliers to form a U (figure 4). Pull the short end of the wire over

figure 4

the pliers to begin a loop (figure 5), and wrap the wire clockwise two or three times to form a collar around the long wire (figure 6). Wraps should start right next to the jaw of the round-nose pliers. Two wraps around the long wire make a collar about ¹⁄₁₆ inch (1.6 mm) long. Remove the loop from the pliers, grasp the inside of the loop with the chain-nose pliers, and bend slightly to center the loop on the long wire (figure 7). Trim off the tail with the flush cutters (figure 8).

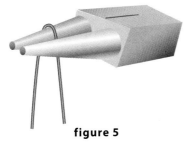

figure 5

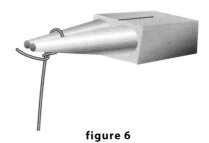

figure 6

figure 7

figure 8

Wire Spiral

Begin with a piece of wire cut to the length specified in the project instructions. Flush cut the working end of the wire. Grasp the wire in round-nose pliers; the end of the wire should not extend past the sides of the jaws (figure 9). Turn the pliers to form a round loop, and then turn slightly past the point where the two wires overlap (figure 10). Switch to chain-nose pliers, and hold the loop between the jaws, with the wire end pointing at your non-dominant hand. Holding it gently in the pliers, pivot the tip of the pliers toward your non-dominant hand, pushing the wire against the loop, to begin forming the spiral (figure 11). Open the pliers slightly, pivot the handles

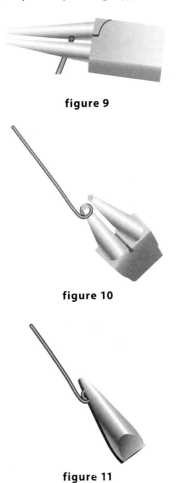

figure 9

figure 10

figure 11

back toward your body, then grasp and turn the wire as before. Each turn of the pliers will add more wire around the outside of the spiral. Continue until the spiral reaches the desired size (figure 12).

figure 12

Twisting

You'll need a drill and an eye-hook mounted on a wall. Start with a single piece of wire in the length specified in the instructions. Feed it through the eye, and center it in the hook. Pull the ends together so the wire is doubled, twist them, insert the ends into a drill, and tightly close the chuck. Pull on the wire firmly, but not so hard that you pull it out of the chuck. Holding the wire taut, slowly start the drill, twisting the wire until each twist is approximately ¹⁄₁₆ inch (1.6 mm) wide—approximately the same width as a size 15° bead. If the ends of the wire break off near the chuck, reinsert them and continue to twist. When done twisting, hold the wire taut, and release the wire from the chuck. Allow the wire to untwist slightly, but not to kink, as you open the drill chuck.

Coiling

You can make coils by hand around a steel mandrel, or form them around a mandrel inserted into a drill. Start with the length of wire specified in the project instructions. Place the wire across the mandrel, with the 1-inch (2.5 cm) tail end close to your body. Hold the tail in your non-dominant hand, and wrap the long wire around the mandrel, away from your body.

- If coiling by hand, continue in the same way until all of the wire is coiled neatly around the rod.

- If coiling with a drill, form a short length of coil by hand, then cut off the short tail or wrap it around the steel mandrel. Insert the end of the mandrel and the short length of the coil into the drill chuck. Be sure the chuck is closed tightly down on both the coil and the mandrel. Hold on to the long length of the wire firmly, and turn on the drill slowly. Run the drill until all of the wire is coiled around the mandrel. Open the chuck, remove the coil and mandrel from the drill chuck, and slide the coil off of the steel mandrel.

Opening and Closing Jump Rings

Jump rings should be opened and closed properly to maintain their shape. Open and close jump rings from side to side, not from front to back or you will distort the ring shape and make it nearly impossible to close.

To open the ring, use two pairs of chain-nose pliers to grasp each side. Pivot the tool held in your dominant hand, pushing that end of the jump ring up past the other end while holding the other end steady (figure 13). To close, use a similar motion, pivoting the pliers back, past the other side, and then push it back and forth until the two ends come together (figure 14). Rocking the jump ring past the point of closure and back hardens the ring slightly, helping to guarantee a tight closure.

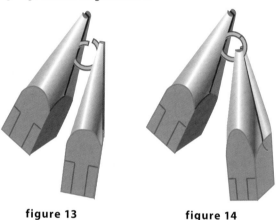

figure 13   **figure 14**

Filing

Files work in only one direction; always push the file forward, away from your body, then reposition it near your body and push it forward again.

Hammering

Strike wire *with the dome* of the hammer to ensure a flat, clean result. If the edge of the hammer strikes the wire, it leaves a distinct, clear mark. To flatten the wire more, continue to tap lightly with the hammer. Don't get carried away, though— wire can be work hardened to the point where it becomes brittle.

Wire Weaving Techniques

Wire weaving consists of attaching a thinner-gauge wire and beads around a heavier-gauge core wire. In this book, I will introduce you to three techniques: flat weaving, dimensional tube weaving, and bezel weaving.

All types of weaving share some standard techniques. Each weave begins with anchor wraps around an outer core wire. A separate, lighter-gauge wire is used to weave beads around the inner and outer core wires, which form the base structure of each design. All three types of weaving end with several wraps around a core wire.

Making a Bead Stop

Cut the weaving wire to the length specified in the project instructions. Use round-nose pliers to grasp the end of the wire, and your non-dominant thumb and index finger to hold the end of the wire. Turn the pliers, and wrap the wire around the tip, forming two tight, consecutive loops (figure 15).

figure 15

Next, string the number of beads specified in the project instructions onto the wire, allowing them to drop down and sit on the bead stop. If you need to add more beads during weaving, cut off the bead stop, add beads, and remake the bead stop.

GLOSSARY OF TERMS

- **Bead stop:** two consecutive wire loops at the end of the weaving wire that prevent strung beads from falling off the wire during weaving.

- **Core wire:** the underlying structural wire, usually 20-gauge or heavier, that forms the shape of the project.

- **Culling beads:** sorting to eliminate misshapen beads.

- **Kinks:** when a wire flips over and forms an unintended loop, it creates a malformation in the wire.

- **Oxidation:** the process by which silver and copper are darkened or colored through chemical exposure. Tarnish also dulls the luster of the metal, but is a naturally occurring discoloration caused by exposure to air, oil, or dirt.

- **Weaving wire:** a lighter gauge wire is used to weave around or between the core wires.

- **Wire tails:** a wire has two ends, or tails. The short tail is the end that remains when the wire is anchored around the structure at the beginning of a woven section. It should be about ¾ inch (1.9 cm) long. Hold the short tail in your non-dominant hand while you begin to weave, and cut it off after completing several rows. The long tail is the remaining length of wire, and is used to weave beads onto the core wire once it's anchored in position.

- **Work hardening:** occurs when the wire is pulled repeatedly or kinked. Too much handling and manipulation results in brittle wire, which is likely to break.

Beginning to Weave

Start every woven section with an anchor wrap. To make the anchor wrap, lay the weaving wire in front of the inner core wire, closest to your body. Always wrap away from your body. Leave a short tail of wire. Make two wraps to complete the anchor wrap (figure 16). If you're right handed, start wrapping on the left and move to the right. If you're left handed, wraps begin on the right and wrap to the left. After weaving several rows, cut off the short tail, and continue weaving with the long tail.

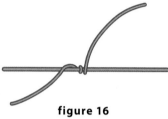

figure 16

Finishing a Weave

When the weaving is complete, wrap the weaving wire twice around the inner core wire and trim off the excess with flush cutters. As a rule, weaving begins and ends on the inner core wire.

Adding Wire

When the original weaving wire breaks or becomes too short to use, wrap twice around the nearest core wire, and trim away the excess. Start a new piece of weaving wire with two anchor wraps around the same core wire, in the same direction, directly adjacent to the two wraps at the end of the previous wire.

TIPS FOR ALL TYPES OF WEAVING
- Handle the core wire as little as possible so as not to distort shape of the structure.
- The project should be flipped over to provide better visibility while working.

Double-Sided Flat Weave

Flat weaves are the most basic way to add beads to a wire structure. Each row sits next to the previous row, filling spaces with color, texture, and a hint of sparkle.

For most of the projects, you'll weave beads on both sides of the core wire structure, creating a double-sided flat weave.

To begin, attach the weaving wire to the core wire by making two anchor wraps where you wish to begin adding beads. Then position the specified number of beads next to the inner core wire. Pull the wire across, and wrap it around the outer core wire one and a half times (figure 17).

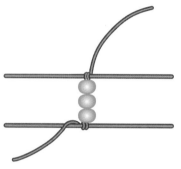

figure 17

Position the same number of beads next to the outer core wire. Pull the wire back across to the inner core wire, and wrap it around one and a half times. This row of beads will sit behind the first row and create a double-sided weave (figure 18).

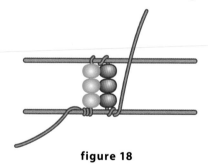

figure 18

Using the number of beads specified in the pattern, position the next row of beads beside the inner core wire. Pull the wire across, and wrap it around the outer core wire one and a half times, positioning this row of beads next to the previous row (figure 19). Continue to repeat the same weaving technique. For each beaded loop, string the number of beads specified in the project instructions. Wire wraps should be positioned side by side, and shouldn't overlap (figure 20).

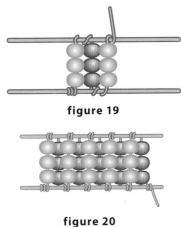

figure 19

figure 20

Single-Sided Flat Weave

For a few projects, you'll weave beads across only the front. This method starts in the same way as a double-sided weave, but on the back of the structure, a bare wire crosses from one core wire to the other, instead of stringing seed beads on both sides.

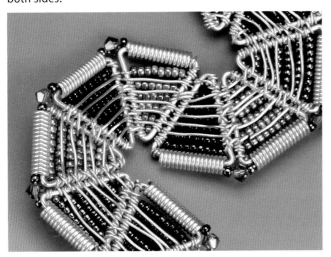

Dimensional Tube Weave

Dimensional weaving fills the spaces in three-dimensional structures to give them color and texture, and to add strength. In dimensional bead weaving, the beads are positioned on the outside of the structure.

Make an anchor wrap around one core wire. Position a seed bead or row of beads next to the first core wire. Pull the weaving wire across the second core wire, and make one full wrap around the second core wire (figure 21).

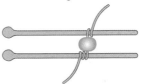

figure 21

Position a seed bead next to the second core wire. Pull the weaving wire across the third core wire, and make one full wrap (figure 22).

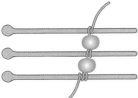

figure 22

Position a seed bead next to the third core wire. Pull the weaving wire across the fourth core wire, and make one full wrap (figure 23).

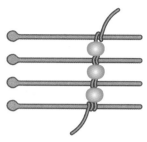

figure 23

Position the core wires into a tube configuration, and hold them in place. Position a seed bead next to the fourth core wire; pull the weaving wire across the first core wire, and make one full wrap (figure 24).

figure 24

Using the number of beads specified for the project, position the next row of beads beside the previous row. Pull the weaving wire across the second core wire, and make one full wrap (figure 25).

figure 25

Continue in the same manner, using the bead and row counts specified for each project (figure 26).

figure 26

Bezel Weave

For this woven wire cage that traps, holds, and displays a round or oval cabochon, the core structure is made with 20-gauge wire; 26-gauge wire serves as the weaving wire.

Use a tape measure to measure the circumference of the cabochon at its largest point (figure 27). The bezel structure is made from multiple loops of wire. Multiply the circumference by the number of loops required to create the bezel—typically five loops—then add 2 inches (5.1 cm) to the sum.

figure 27

Two loops of wire will sit in front of the cabochon, displaying one row of beads. One loop will become the wall that sits along the side of the cabochon. The remaining loops will sit on the back of the cabochon, displaying three more rows of beads. Depending on the depth of the cabochon, it may require more or fewer wire loops.

Mark the core wire 1 inch (2.5 cm) from the end. To create the bezel structure, wrap the wire twice, counterclockwise, around a wooden dowel or round object with a slightly smaller circumference than the cabochon (figure 28).

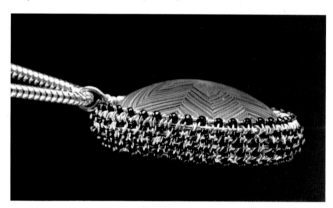

figure 28

Anchor a length of 26-gauge weaving wire at the 1-inch (2.5 cm) mark on the inner core wire. Position a seed bead next to the inner wire, and wrap the weaving wire once clockwise around the second bezel loop (figure 29). Bring the weaving wire back toward the middle of the bezel, and wrap one and a half times around the first bezel loop wire (figure 30). Be careful to maintain the shape of the loops to ensure that the bezel fits the cabochon. Continue weaving clockwise until the two loops of core wire are joined by a continuous row of beads, ending with the weaving wire on the outer (second) loop (figure 31). Leave a gap about the same width as one bead between each bead; do not weave the beads too close together.

figure 29

figure 30

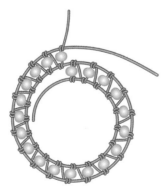

figure 31

To begin the second row of the bezel, feed the weaving wire up between the first and second loops, between beads 1 and 2 of the first loop. This begins the third loop (figure 32).

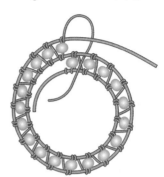

figure 32

Check the size of the bezel by placing the cabochon inside the center of the woven loops. The first woven loop of beads should cover the front edge of the cabochon. If the bezel is too big, slowly pull on the core wire to tighten the loop, and make it slightly smaller. If the bezel is too tight, loosen it by pushing the core wire toward the center, through the beads. If the size is right, set the cabochon aside and begin weaving the second row. Check the fit of the cabochon regularly while creating the bezel.

TIP
Use an awl to create a space between wraps to allow the weaving wire to fit between the beads of the previous row.

To start the next row of the bezel, wrap the weaving wire one and a half times around the next (or third) loop of core wire. Bring the weaving wire under, and then guide it up between beads 2 and 3 of the first row. Continue weaving in the same manner around the bezel (figure 33). Instead of weaving

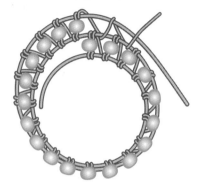

figure 33

between each set of beads, weave between the wraps created while weaving the previous row. As the second row begins to take shape, push it downward to position it beneath the first row. Continue the same pattern, working clockwise, until the second row is complete (figure 34).

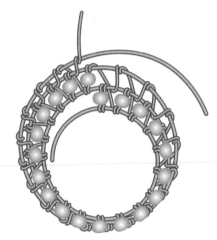

figure 34

The first row of beads sits on the front of the cabochon, and the second loop of the bezel sits along the edge, at a 90° angle to the first row when viewed from the side (figure 35). After completing the second row of beads, insert the cabochon to check the size of the bezel; it should fit inside the second ring. Adjust the size of the second ring as needed. The second ring begins to create the wall of the bezel, which will encase the side of the cabochon.

figure 35

Before weaving the third row, insert the cabochon into the bezel, and weave the last row with the cabochon in position (figure 36). All remaining rows will be constructed in the same way. The last woven loop will sit across the back of the cabochon to hold it in place. When the final loop is woven all the way around to its starting point, weave an additional four rows to lock it in place.

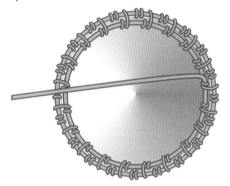

figure 36

Finish the weaving wire with two wraps around the outermost core wire. On the back of the bezel, flush cut the core wire ¾ inch (1.9 cm) from the finishing wraps of weaving wire. Create a flat spiral from the remaining wire. On the front of the bezel, leave a ⅜-inch (1 cm) tail of core wire, and flush cut the weaving wire. Use round-nose pliers to form a bail, rolling a loop toward the back of the cabochon (figure 37).

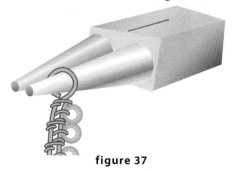

figure 37

Making Findings

To finish necklaces and earrings, you'll need things like clasps or ear wires. Although you can opt to purchase commercially produced components, creating your own findings makes your jewelry 100% handmade.

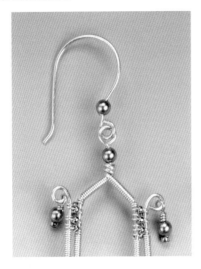

Ear Wires

Cut two 2-inch (5.1 cm) pieces of 20-gauge wire. Use round-nose pliers to form a basic loop on one end of the wire. If desired, slide a bead onto the wire and position it next to the loop. Place the center of the wire on your fine point marker and shape the wire around the pen to form a hook.

Use chain-nose pliers to bend the other end of the hook, flaring it away from the center (figure 38).

figure 38

Jump-Ring Chain

Much of the time, I think a handmade chain gives my designs a unified appearance and looks better than a commercial chain. Making a chain is as simple as linking jump rings.

A 1-in-1 chain consists of one jump ring linked into another single jump ring, linked into a single jump ring, linked into a single jump ring. You get the picture!

For a 2-in-1 chain, the pattern is two rings linked into one, linked into two, linked into one, etc.

Wire Hook Clasp

Flush cut both ends of a 2½-inch (6.4 cm) piece of 16-gauge wire. Using a bench block and chasing hammer, pound the ends into flat paddles (figure 39). Use round-nose pliers to form the flattened paddle ends into small round loops that turn in opposite directions (figure 40).

figure 39

figure 40

Make a bead stop on one end of a 2-foot (61 cm) length of 26-gauge wire. String on 19 size 15° seed beads. Fold the wire in half with seed beads on the right hand side next to the bead stop. Hold the beads in your dominant hand, and wrap two or three times around the 16-gauge wire (figure 41). While holding the beads next to the 16-gauge wire, coil the beads around the clasp (figure 42). Make a few wraps to anchor the wire, and continue wrapping on each side, switching sides frequently, so the seed beads remain centered (figure 43). Wrap all the way to the paddles, and then unwrap twice on each end. Use flush cutters to trim off any remaining 26-gauge wire.

Place the round-nose pliers next to the loop, working where the plier jaws are widest (figure 44). Grasp the wrapped wire, and turn the ends back toward the middle to form a hook (figure 45). Repeat on the opposite side, forming an S shape, with a straight section in the middle wrapped in seed beads (figure 46).

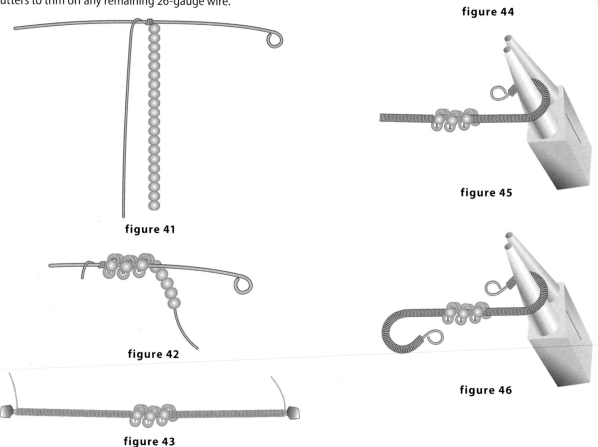

figure 41

figure 42

figure 43

figure 44

figure 45

figure 46

Torch Techniques

Before turning on the micro torch, be sure to read all the safety information. The hottest area of the flame is the internal point inside the cone. That's what you want to use.

Setting Up a Soldering Station

A soldering station is a work area suitable for soldering. Whether this area is temporary or permanent, the micro torch should *always* be turned off when not in use. Emphasize safety: Have a fire extinguisher nearby. Work on a stable, fire-proof surface, in a well-ventilated location, and keep the area clean and uncluttered.

When using a micro torch, placing a cookie sheet under a kiln brick on a sturdy tabletop is an excellent option for a temporary soldering station.

A typical soldering station includes the following tools and supplies:

• Fire extinguisher

• Cookie sheet

• Fire brick

• Micro torch

• Butane fuel canister (stored away from the lighted micro torch)

• Tweezers

• Glass or ceramic bowl of water

• Plastic spray bottle of flux

• Crock pot containing pickle

• Copper tongs

Mixing Pickle

After soldering, the joint will need to be cleaned in hot pickle, so prior to soldering, turn on your crock pot. (If you don't have any made, mix the pickle solution with water according to the manufacturer's directions and pour it in the crock pot.) Once the pickle has been mixed, it is good for a few days. Between uses, make sure you unplug the crock pot. When finished with the solution, allow it to dehydrate, leaving behind crystals, and then use water to rinse away any residue.

> **SAFETY**
> Be very careful with the pickle solution; it is an acid, and can damage your clothes and irritate skin. Always use the copper tongs to place objects into, and remove them from, the solution.

Making Head Pins

A micro torch can be used to make head pins, using 16-gauge wire or smaller. Cut the length and gauge of wire specified for the project. Turn the micro torch on and make sure it stands securely. Grasp the wire near one end with chain-nose pliers. Hold the wire vertically, and lower the other end into the hottest part of the flame (figure 47). Hold it in the flame until the end of the wire melts to form a ball, and then remove it from the flame. (Practice will help you determine the right amount of time needed to form a head on the wire without melting the end off completely.) Place the formed head pins in the pickle solution for a few minutes. After removing the pieces from the pickle, the pieces can be tumbled to add a bit of extra shine if desired.

figure 47

Soldering a Ring

The process described here is specific to soldering wire rings, which requires working with easy solder only.

Cut the length and gauge of silver wire specified for your project and form it into a ring. File the ends of the wire to make them smooth. Rock the ends together until they meet evenly. At this point, file as needed to make sure that there's no space between the ends and that the ring closes tightly.

Put the ring on the fire brick with the joint facing you. Place a pallion of easy solder underneath, making contact with the joint. Spray the solder and the entire ring with a light coat of flux.

Ignite the micro torch. First, preheat the fire brick ¼ inch (6 mm) away from the outside of the ring, using a slow, steady, circular motion. Then heat the ring in a similar manner, without touching the hottest part of the flame to the ring yet. When the ring begins to glow slightly, rotate the torch slowly several times around the ring, focusing the heat closer to the ring.

When the ring and solder are evenly heated, the solder will melt and flow up into the joint. Be careful: If you heat the ring for too long, the silver will melt. After soldering, pick up the ring with tweezers and dip it in the small bowl of water. (This is called quenching. It cools the metal for the next step; otherwise, the temperature difference would cause pickle to sputter and splash.)

Pick up the cooled soldered ring with copper tongs and drop it into the warm pickle solution for a few minutes. Use the copper tongs to remove the ring from the pickle. Rinse the ring with liquid detergent and water.

Finishing the Ring

The soldered ring won't be a perfect circle. To reshape and harden it, place it on a round metal mandrel that fits snugly in the ring. Using a rawhide mallet, hammer with soft blows until the ring is even all around. If desired, give it a high shine by placing it in a rotary tumbler for a few minutes.

Using Liver of Sulfur

Follow the manufacturer's instructions to prepare a small amount of solution. Place the metal or jewelry into the solution until it achieves the desired color, and rinse thoroughly with cool water. Prepared solution can be stored at a warm temperature (less than 160°F [71.1°C]) in a crock pot, but time, light, and oxygen neutralize its potency within a few hours. When the yellow color of the solution disappears, all that's left is mineral-rich water, which can safely be poured down the drain or on a nearby houseplant.

TIPS FOR SUCCESSFUL SOLDERING

- Use as little solder as possible; you need no more than a ¹⁄₁₆-inch (1.6 mm) square pallion.

- Before soldering, clean the solder and the joint with liquid dish detergent.

- Thoroughly flux all solder and wire surfaces to prevent oxidation.

- Oxidation can inhibit solder flow. Joints may need to be filed before soldering.

- All surfaces should reach soldering temperature at the same time.

Rings for Ears & Fingers

SUPPLIES

Silver 20-gauge wire, 14 inches (35.6 cm)

Silver 22-gauge wire, 1½ feet (45.7 cm)

Silver 26-gauge wire, 2 feet (61 cm)

Metallic olive green size 11° seed beads, 5 g

22 olivine crystal bicones, 3 mm

Basic Tool Kit, page 11

0.06-inch (1.6 mm) mandrel

FINISHED SIZE

2¼ (5.7 cm) inches long

TIP
Although the measurements and instructions in each step are for one earring, it's easier to achieve a matched pair if you complete one step, and then immediately repeat that step for the other earring. In other words, make both earrings at the same time.

HIGH RISE EARRINGS

Straight architectural lines define the metropolitan feel of these earrings. Neat stacks of beads hint at lines of windows reflecting back the lights, excitement, and adventures of city life.

1 Wrap all of the 22-gauge wire around the mandrel, forming a coil approximately 1¼ inches (3.2 cm) long. Use flush cutters to trim four separate ¼-inch (6 mm) coils. Set aside. (Do not repeat this step.)

2 Cut two 1⁷⁄₁₆-inch (3.6 cm) pieces of 20-gauge wire. On each, make a mark ⅛ inch (3 mm) from each end. Use chain-nose pliers to make a 90° bend at each mark, bending both ends in the same direction to form prongs.

3 Cut a 14-inch (35.6 cm) piece of 26-gauge wire. Make two anchor wraps onto one of the bent pieces of 20-gauge wire. Trim off the short end of the 26-gauge wire, and leave the long length attached.

4 Insert the short bent ends of both pieces of 20-gauge wire into one of the ¼-inch (6 mm) coils (figure 1). Hold the wires in position with your thumb and index finger. Slide the two wraps of 26-gauge wire up near the coil.

figure 1

TIP
It's important to keep the tension tight, especially while weaving the first few rows, but handle the wire frames carefully. Pulling too hard will distort the sides, which should be kept as straight as possible.

5 Begin a two-sided flat weave by stringing one seed bead, one bicone, and one seed bead. Wrap around the opposite 20-gauge wire, and string four seed beads. Weave back toward the opposite 20-gauge wire, behind the front row of seed beads and bicone. This pattern is used for all of the remaining rows of weaving.

6 After completing the fifth row, add a ¼-inch (6 mm) coil to the other set of prongs. After completing 10 rows, front and back, finish with two wraps around the 20-gauge wire frame, and trim off any remaining weaving wire.

7 Cut a 1¼-inch (3.2 cm) piece of 20-gauge wire. Make a mark ⅛ inch (3 mm) from each end, and one in the center. Using chain-nose pliers, make a 90° bend at the center mark. Next, bend one of the ends at the ⅛-inch (3 mm) mark, toward the center, turning it into a short prong. Bend the opposite end to form a triangle (figure 2). Insert both prongs into the coil at the top of the woven rectangular frame, and squeeze the ends toward each other (figure 3).

figure 2

figure 3

Front (left) and back (right)

8 Make a pair of ear wires using the instructions on page 23, and attach one to the triangle at the top of each earring.

Variation

Silver 20-gauge wire, 2 feet (61 cm)

Silver 26-gauge wire, 6 feet (1.8 m)

2 crystal rivoli stones, 14 mm

Metallic dark green size 15° seed beads, 3 g

44 aquamarine 2XAB crystal bicones, 3 mm

44 head pins, 24 gauge, 1½ inches (3.8 cm)

12 jump rings, 20 gauge, 3 mm inner diameter

2 rubber earring backs

Basic Tool Kit, page 11

FINISHED SIZE

2⅞ inches (7.3 cm) long

TIP

Your earrings will match more closely if you finish one step and then immediately repeat that step to make the second earring. In other words, make both earrings at the same time.

CRYSTAL MAGIC EARRINGS

In an ingenious twist—literally!—the bezel holding each rivoli becomes the stud used to wear the earring.

1 Refer to the instructions that start on page 20 to create a bezel for one of the rivolis. Start with 1 foot of 20-gauge wire and a 3-foot (0.91 m) piece of 26-gauge wire. On the first row, you will weave 19 seed beads around the front edge of the rivoli. Next, weave two bare wire rows that sit along the side, and then two rows on the back to lock the rivoli in position. Trim the wire on the front of the stone to ⅜ inch (1 cm), and use round-nose pliers to form a simple round loop positioned at

Back

the bottom of the earring (figure 1). Complete the fifth row on the back, directly across from the loop. At the back of the rivoli, trim the 20-gauge wire to ⅜ inch (1 cm) long, and bend it so it points away from the rivoli to form the earring post (figure 2).

2 Make 22 dangles for each earrings—a total of 44 dangles. Each dangle is comprised of a size 15° seed bead, a 3-mm crystal, and a second size 15° seed bead strung onto a head pin, with a small wire-wrapped loop above the beads.

3 Open the loop on one of the rivolis, insert four dangles into the loop, and close the loop. Slide three dangles onto an empty jump ring, slide the ring through the loop between the dangles, and close the ring. Position two dangles on one side of the jump rings, and one dangle on the other side of the ring, and add another jump ring containing three dangles. Repeat four more times, to add a total of six jump rings and 22 dangles to create a fringe at the bottom of the earring (figure 3).

figure 1

figure 2

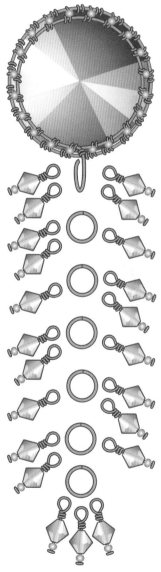

figure 3

Variation

SUPPLIES

Silver 20-gauge wire, 2 feet (61 cm)

Silver 26-gauge wire, 10 feet (3 m)

Purple metallic iris size 15° seed beads, 3 g

4 rose crystal bicones, 3 mm

4 silver jump rings, 18 gauge, 3 mm inner diameter

4 silver head pins, 24 gauge, 1½ inches (3.8 cm)

Basic Tool Kit, page 11

0.03-inch (0.08 mm) mandrel

FINISHED SIZE

2½ inches (6.4 cm)

TIP
Your earrings will match more closely if you finish one step and then immediately repeat that step to make the second earring. In other words, make both earrings at the same time.

QUASAR EARRINGS

Form coils into retro-chic starbursts that become the focal element in earrings that playfully mix nuclear-age and classic design motifs.

Top Element

1 Cut two pieces of 20-gauge wire, each 3 inches (7.6 cm) long. Use round-nose pliers to make a small loop at the end of one of the wires. Mark the other wire ½ inch (1.3 cm) from the end. Hold the ½-inch (1.3 cm) tail, and wrap twice around the other wire. Trim off the short tail, at the top. Pull the two wires apart to form a V beneath the loop (figure 1).

figure 1

2 Cut an 8-inch (20.3 cm) piece of 26-gauge wire, and anchor wrap it twice around one of the 20-gauge wires. Begin a double-sided flat weave with a single-bead row. For the next five rows, add one bead for each row, front and back, until six rows are complete. Make two wraps around the nearest 20-gauge wire, and trim off any remaining weaving wire (figure 2).

figure 2

3 Trim the 20-gauge wires ⅜ inch (1 cm) from the last row of beads. On each one, use round-nose pliers to form a simple loop that rolls up toward the top of the triangle.

Bottom Element

4 Coil 6 feet (1.8 m) of 26-gauge wire around the mandrel. Cut seven coils, each ½ inch (1.3 cm) long.

5 Cut a 4-inch (10.2 cm) piece of 20-gauge wire and a 15-inch (38.1 cm) piece of 26-gauge wire. Anchor wrap the 26-gauge wire around the 20-gauge wire and trim off the short tail.

6 Slide a size 15° seed bead, a ½-inch (1.3 cm) coil, and another size 15° seed bead onto the wire. Arch the coil, pulling the weaving wire back toward the 20-gauge wire to form it into a loop. Hold the shaped loop in place, and wrap the weaving wire around the 20-gauge wire (figure 3). Make six more loops in the same way, weaving straight along the wire, and leave the weaving wire attached.

figure 3

7 Center the group of loops in the middle of the 20-gauge wire. Pull the ends of the 20-gauge wire toward each other and cross them, keeping the coiled loops at the middle and forming a teardrop-shaped loop. Wrap the weaving wire twice around the spot where the two wires cross, then wrap two more times (figure 4). You've created the starburst, but you're not finished with the bottom element yet.

figure 4

8 Pull the ends of the 20-gauge wire apart to form a V. Weave the same pattern as used for the top element,

making six rows, front and back. Wrap twice, and trim off any remaining weaving wire. Trim each 20-gauge wire to ⅜ inch (1 cm), and use round-nose pliers to make a round loop of each end, rolling back out and down toward the starburst.

Finish

9 Use two pairs of chain-nose pliers to open the jump rings. Use one ring to join the loops of the top and bottom elements.

10 Make a pair of ear wires following the instructions on page 23, and attach them to the loop on top of the upper triangle.

11 Finally, make the dangles. String one size 15° seed bead, a 3-mm bicone, and one more seed bead onto a head pin, then form a loop above the top bead, but don't close it yet. Attach the loop to the loop at the top of the lower element, and then complete the dangle with a wire-wrapped loop. Repeat on the other side of the earring.

Variation

34

Silver 20-gauge wire, 6 inches
(15.2 cm)

Silver 22-gauge wire, 20 inches
(50.8 cm)

Silver 26-gauge wire, 8 feet (2.5 m)

Green iris dark plum size 15° round
3-cut seed beads, 2 g

1 crystal AB rivoli stone, 14 mm

Basic Tool Kit, page 11

0.03-inch (0.8 mm) mandrel

Weave the Basket

1 Fold 20 inches (50.8 cm) of silver
22-gauge wire in half in such a way that
the U at the center is about as wide as a
size 15° seed bead. Anchor wrap a 4-foot
(1.2 m) piece of 26-gauge wire, and slide
the wrap next to the fold, on the side
closest to you. String one seed bead,
and begin a single sided flat weave until
you've completed a total of three rows.

2 Use chain-nose pliers to grasp the U,
and shape the wire into a curved hook
(figure 1). Weave six more rows with
a single bead on one side and a bare
wire across the back. As you weave,
continue to shape the 22-gauge wire
into a spiral shape.

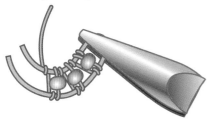

figure 1

THE RING

**This cocktail ring hints at the depth of a crystal rivoli
beneath the texture of woven seed beads.**

3 After the ninth row, the weaving will come almost full circle. Weave the 10th row and wrap underneath the inner 22-gauge wire. Come up between the first and second bead, and pull the wire across both of the 22-gauge wires (figure 2). The wire is now positioned to begin weaving the second spiral.

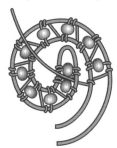

figure 2

4 On every other bead in the second spiral, add the bead on the front, wrap around the outer wire, wrap the bare wire across the bottom, wrap once around the inner wire, and then wrap once around the outer wire of the previous spiral. String the next bead, bring the wire back to the outer 22-gauge wire, and wrap the next row without wrapping around the previous spiral. Weave 16 bead rows to complete the second spiral. Push your thumb up into the spiral to begin to form it into a basket shape as you weave the second row.

5 Continue to shape the 22-gauge wire into a spiral, and weave a third row that sits perpendicular to the second row, to create a wall. Be sure to anchor the previous row to the current row after weaving on every other bead. The third row will create enough depth for the rivoli to nest down inside of the basket (figure 3).

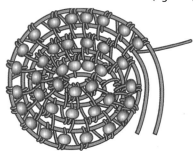

figure 3

6 Test the rivoli to make sure it fits in the basket. Set the rivoli aside. Weave a fourth row and then a fifth, and anchor the weaving to the previous spiral.

7 Use chain-nose pliers to make a 90° bend next to the last woven row. Make a mark 3/16 inch (5 mm) from the bend, and mark 3/16 inch (5 mm) from the first mark. Position the round-nose pliers near the second mark, and pull the wire around to form a small prong. At the second mark, make a 90° bend to position the 22-gauge wire next to the spiral (figure 4).

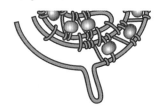

figure 4

8 Wrap the weaving wire four times around the inner 22-gauge wire to bridge the gap below the prong. Weave five more single bead rows. Repeat step 7 to make a second prong. Weave five more rows, and then make a third prong. Weave about five beads after the last prong, then wrap the outer 22-gauge wire twice around the inner 22-gauge wire. Trim off the wrapped wire, and then trim the remaining wire 1/4 inch (6 mm) beyond the wraps. Use round-nose pliers to form the short end into a tight loop (figure 5).

figure 5

9 Insert the rivoli face down into the basket. Use chain-nose pliers to fold each of the three prongs down across the back of the rivoli, along with the small end loop made in the previous step (figure 6).

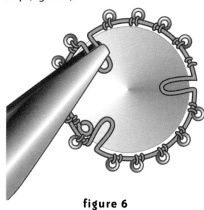

figure 6

Ring Band

10 Coil 4 feet (1.2 m) of silver 26-gauge wire around the mandrel. Use the following formula to determine the correct measurements for your ring band:
- Measure your finger size.
- Subtract 3/4 inch (1.9 cm) from the size.
- Add 3/16 inch (5 mm) to the last total.

This total is the proper coil length for your ring band. Cut two coils of that length.

11 Cut two 3-inch (7.6 cm) pieces of 20-gauge wire. Mark each one 3/4 inch (1.9 cm) from one end. Set aside for the time being. Cut two pieces of 26-gauge wire, each 6 inches (15.2 cm) long. Make a bead stop at the end of each one, and string 20 seed beads onto each.

12 Wrap one of the 6-inch (15.2 cm) pieces of 26-gauge wire twice around both pieces of 20-gauge wire, and position the wraps at the marks. Use chain-nose pliers to bend the 20-gauge wires at an angle to form a V. Begin a two-sided flat weave as follows. Start with a single-bead row, and increase each row by one bead for a total of four rows. At the end of the last row, wrap twice around the 20-gauge frame, and trim off any remaining weaving wire (figure 7).

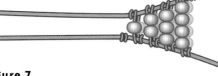

figure 7

13 Trim both 20-gauge wires ¼ inch (6 mm) past the woven section. Use round-nose pliers to form each end into a simple loop.

14 Slide the coils cut in step 10 onto the 20-gauge wires. Wrap the second 6-inch (15.2 cm) piece of 26-gauge wire around both pieces of 20-gauge wire, next to the ends of the coils. Bend the two wires apart to make space to start the first single-bead row of weaving. Start with a single bead row, then add one bead to each row for a total of four rows, front and back. At the end of the last row, wrap twice around the 20-gauge wire and trim off any remaining weaving wire. Undo the two wraps from the beginning of the woven section and trim off the starting tail wire (figure 8).

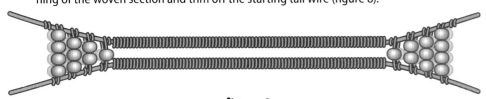

figure 8

15 Trim both 20-gauge wires ¼ inch (6 mm) past the woven section. Use round-nose pliers to form each end into a simple loop.

16 Open the loops at each end of the band with chain-nose pliers. Attach both sides of one end of the band through the 22-gauge wire at the bottom of the woven basket holding the rivoli. Use chain-nose pliers to close each loop securely. Shape the band around a ring mandrel or other round object. Attach both ends of the other end of the band through the opposite side of the basket in the same way, and use chain-nose pliers to close the loops.

Variation

TIP

Your earrings will match more
closely if you finish one step and
then immediately repeat that step
to make the second earring. In
other words, make both earrings at
the same time.

LA FIESTA EARRINGS

With a shape reminiscent of the arcades along a Mexican plaza, these
festive earrings combine straight lines and graceful curves outlined in
a gentle bow of pearls.

1 Cut two 5-inch (12.7 cm) pieces of 20-gauge wire, and mark both pieces 2 inches (5.1 cm) from one end.

2 Cut a 20-inch (50.8 cm) piece of 26-gauge weaving wire. Make a bead stop on one end. String 72 seed beads onto the wire, which will total roughly 3⅛ inches (8 cm) of strung beads.

3 Wrap the weaving wire three times around the two pieces of 20-gauge wire, at the 2-inch (5.1 cm) mark. These anchor wraps will be removed later. Wrap once around the wire nearest to you, which will be the outer wire of the earring. Pull the wires apart slightly to make a gap wide enough to fit a single seed bead.

4 Start a two-sided flat weave by placing a seed bead next to the nearest (outer) wire and make one complete wrap around the inner wire. Add one seed bead on the back, behind the first seed bead, and wrap back across to the outer wire.

TIP

The wraps on the inner wire will lie much closer together than the outer wire's wraps, which will spread apart as you add rows.

5 As you weave in this step, push your thumb along the inside of the outer wire to curve it away from the inner wire. Continue the two-sided flat weave, making each row one bead longer than the previous row, until both sides of the sixth row are complete (figure 1). The sixth row is the widest portion of the curve, the one at the very bottom of the finished earring. From this point, weave each row one bead shorter than the previous row as you curve the outer wire back toward the inner wire. Weave until the curve tapers back down to a single bead row. Anchor wrap twice around the outer wire.

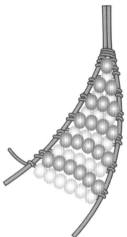

figure 1

6 String two seed beads, one pearl, and two more seed beads onto the wire. Bring the wire behind the outer 20-gauge wire, up between the 10th and 11th rows (figure 2). Pull the wire

figure 2

down, positioning the pearl on the edge of the outer wire. Repeat ten times, wrapping between each row, to add a total of 11 pearls across the bottom of the curve. Finish by wrapping twice around the outer wire between the first and second rows, and trim off any remaining wire. Unwrap the anchor wraps at the beginning of the woven section, and trim off the excess wire (figure 3).

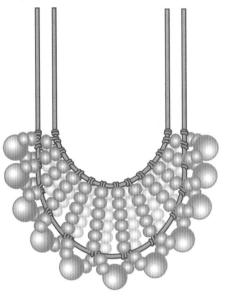

figure 3

7 Coil 4 feet 8 inches (1.5 m) of 26-gauge wire around the mandrel. Cut two ⅜-inch (1 cm) and two ¼-inch (6 mm) sections of coil. Cut two 8-inch (20.3 cm) pieces of 26-gauge wire. Coil one of the pieces around the mandrel 25 times, to make a ⅜-inch (1 cm) section of coil. Trim off the short tail and leave the long portion of the wire intact. Repeat with the second 8-inch (20.3 cm) piece of wire.

8 Slide one of the ⅜-inch (1 cm) coils onto the inner 20-gauge wire. Slide one of the ⅜-inch (1 cm) coils with attached wire onto the outer wire. Push the tip of your chain-nose pliers between the two 20-gauge wires to make a space wide enough for a seed bead.

9 Position one seed bead between the two 20-gauge wires and wrap around the inner wire one-and-a-half times. Wrap back across to the outer wire, and add a seed bead. Repeat two more times, until three seed beads are wrapped to the frame and the weaving wire is wrapped around the outer 20-gauge wire. Trim off the excess weaving wire. Add coils and weave three seed beads onto the opposite side of the wirework.

10 On each side, measure the outer 20-gauge wire ⅜-inch (1 cm) from the anchor wraps and trim off any remaining wire. *Leave the inner wire untrimmed!* Use round-nose pliers to form the ⅜-inch (1 cm) section into a simple round loop.

11 Use chain-nose pliers to grasp the inner wire just above the woven section and bend the wire at an angle, toward the center. Repeat on the opposite side of the beadwork.

12 Slide a ¼-inch (6 mm) coil onto each of the inner wires. Use chain-nose pliers to grasp one of the wires right above the coil. Bend one wire straight up in the middle of the earring, away from the curve. Wrap the other wire around three times, right next to the bend, and trim the wire close to the wraps. Leave the straight wire untrimmed (figure 4).

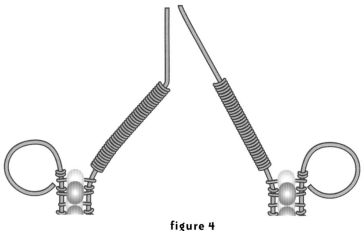

figure 4

13 Slide a pearl onto the straight section of 20-gauge wire. Trim the wire ⅜ inch (1 cm) above the pearl. Use round-nose pliers to form the ⅜-inch (1 cm) section into a basic round loop.

14 Make a pair of ear wires, referring to the instructions on page 23, adding a pearl onto the wire. Attach the ear wires to the loop at the top of the earring.

15 Make a wire-wrapped dangle by stringing one seed bead and a pearl onto a head pin. Make a wrapped loop above the two beads. Use chain-nose pliers to open one of the side loops formed in step 10. Slide the beaded dangle into the loop, and close the loop. Repeat, adding a dangle to the opposite side of the earring.

Variations

Bracelets & Cuffs

From big and bold to classically understated, this section offers a wide range of adornment for your wrist.

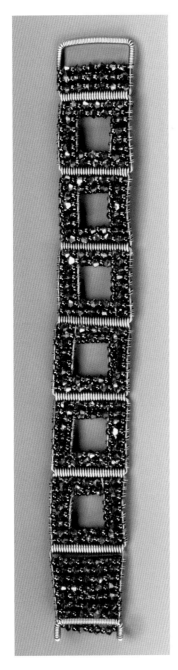

CARRÉ BRACELET

Hinged windows are framed in intricate patterns of crystals and seed beads, joined by wire coils, and finished with a custom clasp.

Prepare the Coils

1 Coil 9 feet (2.7 m) of 20-gauge wire around the 0.08-inch (2.1 mm) mandrel. Trim seven coils, each ¾ inch (1.9 cm) long.

2 Coil 3 feet (1 m) of 24-gauge wire around the 0.04-inch (1 mm) mandrel. Trim two coils, each 1⅜ inches (3.5 cm) long.

Make the Squares

You'll make a number of linked squares with a total length close to—but shorter than—the bracelet length you want. Later, you'll add length when you add the clasp hook, thereby customizing the length of the bracelet. Refer to the box on page 43 for specific size details.

3 For the first square, cut two pieces of 18-gauge wire, each 1⅝ inches long. Make a mark ⅜ inch (1 cm) from both ends of the two wires. Use chain-nose pliers to make a 90° bend at each mark, in the same direction (figure 1). The finished pieces will look like staples.

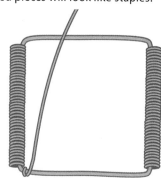

figure 1

4 Cut an 18-inch (45.7 cm) piece of 26-gauge wire. Anchor wrap the wire onto one of the staples made in step 3. Cut off the short tail. Insert the short ends of the two staples into two of the coils made in step 1, forming a square frame.

5 Position the anchor-wrapped weaving wire on the bottom of the square. Start with a size 11° seed bead, and string an alternating pattern of one seed bead and one 3-mm bicone crystal, until there are six seed beads and five bicones strung on the wire. This is the front pattern for the two-sided flat weave. The back row is comprised of 13 size 11° seed beads. Weave two rows, front and back.

6 Cut a ¾-inch (1.9 cm) piece of 18-gauge wire. Slide the end in between the front and back rows of weaving, and hold it in position next to the second seed bead (figure 2). String one size 11° seed bead, one 3-mm bicone, and one size 11° seed bead, and make one complete wrap around the ¾-inch (1.9 cm) piece of 18-gauge wire. String three size 11° seed beads, pull the wire back to the outside of the square, and make one complete wrap around the frame wire (figure 3). Complete three more rows using the same pattern, until you've completed four short rows, front and back. Leave the weaving wire in place.

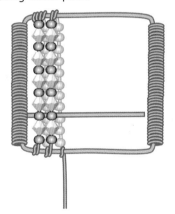

figure 2

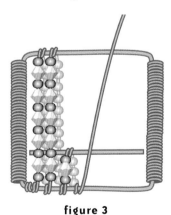

figure 3

7 Cut a 10-inch (25.4 cm) piece of 26-gauge wire, and a ¾-inch (1.9 cm) piece of 18-gauge wire. Anchor wrap the 26-gauge wire twice around the short piece of 18-gauge wire, and trim off the short tail. Slide the end between the front and back rows of beads, and hold the wire in position next to the second seed bead on the top side of the square (figure 4). String a size 11° seed bead, a 3-mm bicone, and a size 11° seed bead onto the weaving wire, and make one complete wrap around the outer frame wire. String three size 11° seed beads, and make one complete wrap around the short 18-gauge wire. Continue a two-sided flat weave that uses the same pattern until you've completed four rows, and trim off the weaving wire (figure 5).

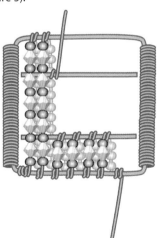

figure 4

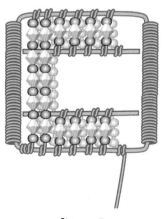

figure 5

SUPPLIES

Silver 18-gauge wire, 7 feet (2.1 m)

Silver 20-gauge, 9 feet (2.7 m)

Silver 24-gauge wire, 3½ feet (1 m)

Silver 26-gauge wire, 23 feet (7 m)

Burgundy metallic size 11° seed beads, 20 g

235 rose satin crystal bicones, 3 mm

Basic Tool Kit, page 11

Mandrels

    0.08 inch (2.1 mm)

    0.04 inch (1 mm)

FINISHED SIZE

6½ inches (6.5 cm)

HOW MANY LINKS?

- Make 5 linked squares for a finished bracelet shorter than 6½ inches (16.5 cm).

- Make 6 linked squares for a finished bracelet that's between 6½ and 7 inches (16.5 and 17.8 cm) long.

- Make 7 linked squares for a finished bracelet that's between 7 and 7½ inches (17.8 and 19 cm) long.

- Make eight squares for a finished bracelet that's between 7½ and 8 inches (19 and 20.3 cm) long.

- Make nine squares for a finished bracelet longer than 8 inches (20.3 cm).

8 String the same pattern used for the first two rows onto the weaving wire from step 6. Weave two rows, front and back, that match the first rows of the square. After the back of the second row is complete, wrap twice around the square frame, and trim off any remaining weaving wire.

9 To start the next square, make two more staples as described in step 3 and slide their short ends into the coil on one side of the first square (figure 6). Anchor wrap a new 18-inch (45.7-cm) piece of 26-gauge wire on the bottom half of the new square. Repeat the same stringing pattern used for the first square. Weave the number of squares described in the How Many Links box (page 43) for your desired size, linking each into the previously made square.

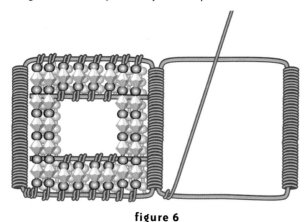

figure 6

Make the Clasp Loop

10 Cut a 2⅝-inch (6.7 cm) piece of 18-gauge wire. Mark the wire ⅝ inch (1.6 cm) from one end. Slide on one of the coils completed in step 2, and position it next to the mark. Mark the coil ¼ inch (6 mm) from each end. Use chain-nose pliers to bend both the 18-gauge wire and the coil 90° at the ¼-inch (6 mm) marks, in the same direction. Mark the 18-gauge wire ¼ inch (6 mm) from the ends of the coils. Use chain-nose pliers to make a 90° bend at each mark, to form a rectangle (figure 7). Wrap a 1-foot (30.5 cm) piece of 26-gauge wire

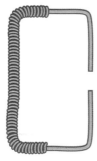

figure 7

around the 18-gauge wire, next to one of the coils. To attach the loop to the bracelet, slide the two ends into the coils of an end square.

11 Weave three rows, front and back, using the same pattern as the body of the bracelet (figure 8). After the third row is complete, wrap twice, and trim off any remaining weaving wire.

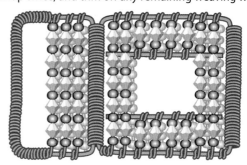

figure 8

Back

Make the Clasp Hook

Here's where you make final adjustments to the length of the beadwork to achieve the fit you want. Measure what you've made so far. For each ¼ inch (6 mm) of additional length desired, add ½ inch (13 mm) to the 4⅛ inches (10.5 cm) described in step 12 below, and weave extra rows. If the bracelet is too long, subtract ½ inch (1.3 cm) from the measurement in step 12, and weave fewer rows.

12 For a 6½-inch (16.5 cm) bracelet, cut a 4⅛ (10.5 cm) piece of 18-gauge wire. Make a mark ⅜ inch (1 cm) from one end, and place a second mark 1 inch (2.5 cm) from the first mark. Slide on the remaining coil finished in step 2, and position it next to the second mark on the 18-gauge wire. Mark the coil ⅜ inch (1 cm) from each end. Use chain-nose pliers to bend both the coil and the wire 90° at the ⅜-inch (1 cm) marks. Make another 90° bend at the other ⅜-inch (1 cm) mark.

13 Use chain-nose pliers to grasp the wire near the end of the coil, and bend the wire and coil close to 90°, to form it into a hook. Next, bend the bare 18-gauge wire at the ⅜-inch (1 cm) mark, and bend the end parallel with the coil at the end (figure 9).

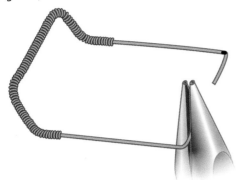

figure 9

14 Anchor wrap a 2½-foot (76.2-cm) piece of 26-gauge wire next to the coil. Slide the ⅜-inch (1 cm) ends into the coil on the square at the end of the bracelet. Slide the weaving wire up next to the body of the bracelet. Begin a two-sided flat weave, using in the first several row the same pattern as in the bracelet's body. Continue to weave until there's enough room left for four rows. To make the next few rows slightly narrower, weave two rows with a seed bead, a crystal, a seed bead, a crystal, two seed beads, a crystal, a seed bead, a crystal, and a seed bead. On the back of these two rows, use as many seed beads as needed to fill the space between the 18-gauge wires.

15 Weave the last two rows with an alternating pattern of a seed bead, a bicone, a seed bead, a bicone, a seed bead, a bicone, and a seed bead on the front, and as many seed beads as needed across the back. After you've woven the last row, wrap the weaving wire twice around the nearest 18-gauge wire, and trim off any remaining wire.

Variation

SUPPLIES

Silver 16-gauge wire, 1 foot (30.5 cm)

Silver 20-gauge wire, 10 feet (3 m)

Silver 24-gauge wire, 30 feet (9.1 m)

Size 15° purple and aqua round seed beads, 5 g

Basic Tool Kit, page 11

³/₃₂-inch (2.4 mm) center punch

0.06-inch (1.6 mm) mandrel

FINISHED SIZE

6½ inches (6.5 cm) long

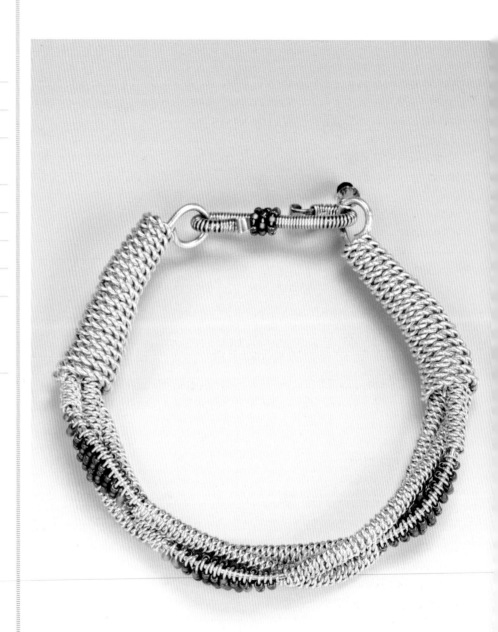

Twist and Coil the Wire

1 Twist a 24-foot (7.3 m) piece of 24-gauge wire. Next, twist a 6½-foot (2 m) piece of 20-gauge wire.

2 Coil the twisted 24-gauge wire around the mandrel. Cut the coil into 5-inch (12.7 cm) sections.

Weave the Diamonds

3 Cut six pieces of 20-gauge wire, each 7 inches (17.8 cm) long. Mark two pieces 3 inches (7.6 cm) from one end, mark two pieces 2 inches (5.1 cm) from one end, and mark the remaining two pieces 4 inches (10.2 cm) from one end.

BRAIDS BRACELET

When they say diamonds are a girl's best friend, they mean the gemstone—but what about the shape? In this bracelet, colorful beaded diamonds intertwine around the wrist, catching the attention of admirers.

4 Line up the two wires marked at 3 inches (7.6 cm). Wrap a 13-inch (33 cm) piece of 24-gauge wire twice around the marks on the two wires; you'll remove these wraps later. Wrap the wire twice around the wire nearest to your body. Use chain-nose pliers to bend each wire until it forms a V wide enough to fit a seed bead. Begin a two-sided flat weave as follows. Add one bead to each row until you reach row 6. After weaving the back of row 6, which is six beads wide, use chain-nose pliers to bend both 20-gauge wires back toward the middle, to form a diamond shape. Weave five beads across both sides of row 7. Taper down one bead for each row until you've woven both sides of row 11, which is a single-bead row. Wrap twice around the wire nearest your body, and trim off the remaining weaving wire (figure 1). Unwrap the two wraps from the beginning of the weaving, and trim off that tail as well.

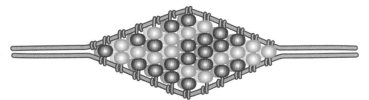

figure 1

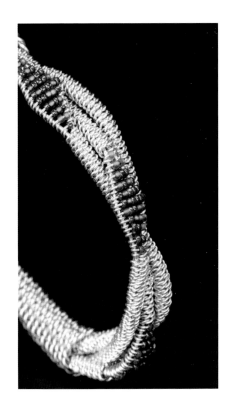

5 Weave two more diamonds in the same way, starting the diamond at 2 inches (5.1 cm) on the pair of wires marked at that spot, and at 4 inches (10.2 cm) on the other pair.

Form the Braids

6 The length of coil needed is determined by the desired finished size of the bracelet. For a bracelet 6 inches (15.2 cm) long, mark the 20-gauge wire 1½ inches (3.8 cm) from the ends of the wires. Measure the distance from the mark to the diamond, and cut the coil to the length from the side of the diamond to the mark. Repeat on the other side.

For every ¼ inch (6 mm) of additional length desired, subtract ⅛ inch (3 mm) from 1½ inches (3.8 cm), mark the wire, measure the distance from the mark to the diamond, and cut the coil to the measurement from the diamond and the mark. On the two off-center diamond assemblies, the coils will be different lengths, one short and one long (figure 2).

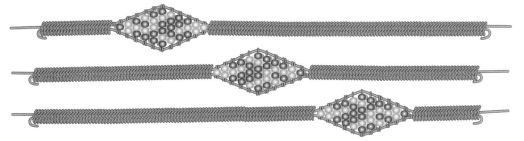

figure 2

7 Each coil has two wires emerging from the end. Cut one of the two wires to ¼ inch (6 mm). Use chain-nose pliers to fold each ¼-inch (6 mm) piece over the ends of the coil to lock it in position, and leave the other wire in place (figure 3).

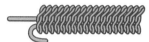

figure 3

8 Cut two pieces of 16-gauge wire, each 3 inches (7.6 cm) long. Form a loop 1 inch (2.5 cm) from the end of one wire, wrapping one side around the other like a twist-tie. Wrap the long end pieces around the twisted loop, making sure that the diamond centered along its length of coil is positioned between the others (figure 4). Don't bother making the ends look neat and tidy since they'll be hidden inside the cones at the ends. Make a second twist-tie loop, and set it aside.

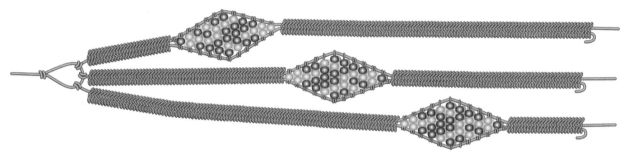

figure 4

9 Braid the strands three times, without twisting or pulling the coils over the top of the diamonds. After braiding, arrange, pull together, and reshape the braids until the coils line up at the other end (figure 5). Twist each of the wires around the second twist-tie loop made in step 8.

figure 5

Shape the Cones

10 Cut two 17-inch (43.2 cm) pieces of twisted 20-gauge wire. Coil each wire around the center punch, working from the wide end to the narrow end and keeping each wrap tight against the previous one. Slide the completed coil off of the center punch and trim each end neatly.

Finish the Ends

11 Slide a wire cone on each side, wide end first, over one the 16-gauge loops attached to the end of the braid, covering the very ends of the coils. Use round-nose pliers to form a basic round loop large enough to fit the clasp.

12 Use the instructions starting on page 23 to make a wire hook clasp, but cut the 16-gauge wire 2¼ inches (5.7 cm) instead of 2½ inches (6.4 cm). Attach the clasp to one round loop emerging from one of the cones, and use the other loop as the other half of the clasp.

INFINITY BRACELET

**Curved coils encase sparkling crystals in an unmistakably modern bracelet,
heavy on metal with bright hints of color and sparkle.**

Silver 18-gauge wire, 2½ feet
(76.2 cm)

Silver 24-gauge wire, 11 feet (3.3 m)

Silver 26-gauge wire, 17½ feet
(5.3 m)

Pale golden orange size 11° round seed
beads, 15 g

22 Bali silver daisy spacers, 4 mm

22 faceted orange rondels,
4 x 6 mm

Basic Tool kit, page 11

0.03-inch (0.8 mm) mandrel

FINISHED SIZE

6½ inches (16.5 cm) long

HOW MANY COILS?

A bracelet 6½ to 6¾ inches
(16.5 to 17.1 cm) long requires 20
to 23 coils. For each ¼ inch (6 mm)
of additional length desired, add
approximately three coils. For
example, a bracelet 8½ to 8¾ inches
(21.6 to 22.2 cm) long will need
approximately 44 to 47 coils.

Begin the Loop End

1 Cut a 9½-inch (24.1-cm) length of
24-gauge wire. Coil it 50 times around
a 24-inch (61-cm) piece of 18-gauge
wire, until the coil is about 1 inch
(2.5 cm) long. Trim off the short tail
at the beginning of the coil. Slide the
coil to the center of the 18-gauge wire,
and form the center of the wire into a
teardrop with the ends crossed at the
top. Wrap the 24-gauge wire three
times around both wires to secure
them in place (figure 1). From this
point on, each end will be referred as a
separate wire.

figure 1

2 Spread the two wires apart. Wrap
the weaving wire twice around the
wire nearest to your body. Begin a
two-sided flat weave with a single
bead row, front and back. Weave three
more rows, making each row one bead
longer than the previous row, until
four rows are complete. For rows 5
through 8, the pattern for the front
is two size 11° seed beads, one Bali

spacer, and two seed beads (figure 2).
The pattern for the back is five seed
beads for all rows.

figure 2

Weave the Body

3 Coil 17½ feet of 26-gauge wire around
the mandrel. Trim the coil into ⅝-inch
(1.6 cm) sections.

The pattern for the body of the bracelet
is the same from one end to the other.
At row 9, string a ⅝-inch (1.6 cm) coil.
Pull the weaving wire across the front of
the bracelet, curving the coil as it goes
from one side to the other (figure 3). All
remaining odd numbered rows of the
body will be woven with a coil. Weave
six seed beads across the back on this
row, *as well as on all remaining rows in
the body of the bracelet.*

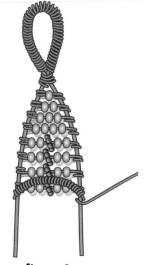

figure 3

4 For row 10, and all the even numbered rows in the rest of the body, the bead pattern is one size 11° seed bead, a Bali spacer, a rondel, a Bali spacer, and a seed bead. Continue the body pattern by weaving six seed beads across the back (figure 4).

figure 4

5 Repeat the patterns in steps 3 and 4 until the body of the bracelet reaches the desired number of rows.

Weave the Hook End

6 After the body is complete, weave the same pattern as rows 1 through 8 of the loop end, but in reverse to taper back down to a single bead.

7 Wrap one of the 18-gauge wires twice around the other, and trim the tail of the wrapped wire.

8 Wrap the remaining weaving wire around the single 18-gauge wire 75 times to make a coil about 1½ inches (3.8 cm) long. Slide the coil toward the bracelet until a space ¹⁄₁₆ inch (1.6 mm) wide remains between the coil and the 18-gauge wraps. Fold the 18-gauge wire at the center of the coil, and bring the sides close together. As shown in figure 5, hold both wires with chain-nose pliers, and wrap the wire twice in the ¹⁄₁₆-inch (1.6-mm) gap at the base of the coil (figure 5).

figure 5

9 Trim off the remaining 18-gauge wire. Use round-nose pliers to form a hook that extends over the wraps made at the very end of step 8. Use chain-nose pliers to bend the end of the hook slightly upwards (figure 6).

figure 6

10 Shape the bracelet into a curve until it fits well around your wrist and the clasp can be opened and closed easily.

Variation

ARTHURIAN CUFF

Wire armor, almost like chain mail, encases a woven base of pearls and seed beads that could have been worn by Guinevere herself.

Prepare the Coils

1 For the decorative crystal band, coil 16 inches (40.6 cm) of 24-gauge wire around the 0.06-inch (1.6 mm) mandrel, then cut the coil into two pieces, each ½ inch (1.3 cm) long.

2 Coil 3 feet (91.4 cm) of 24-gauge wire around the 0.08-inch (2.1 mm) mandrel. Cut this coil into one ⅞-inch (2.2 cm) piece and one ⅝-inch (1.6 cm) piece to use later for the loop and hook ends of the clasp.

3 Coil 18 inches (45.7 cm) of 24-gauge wire around the 0.04-inch (1 mm) mandrel, and cut two coils ¼-inch (6 mm) long, and two other coils ⅜-inch (1 cm) long, which will be used later for the clasp.

4 Calculate the amount of wire needed for the coil loops as follows. This depends on the *finished inner diameter* of the bracelet.

- Bracelets from 6 to 6½ inches (15.2–16.5 cm) require 56 feet (4.9 m) of coil, and 14 side rows.

- Bracelets 7 to 7½ inches (17.8–19 cm) use 72 feet (22 m) of coil, and 15 side rows.

- Bracelets larger than 8 inches (20.3 cm) require 80 feet (24.3 m) of coil, and 16 or more side rows.

5 Coil the required amount of 26-gauge wire around the 0.03-inch (0.8 mm) mandrel, then cut the finished coils into ¾-inch (1.9 cm) lengths.

Decorative Crystal Band

6 Cut two pieces of 20-gauge wire, each 4¼ inches (11.4 cm) long. Mark both pieces 1 inch (2.5 cm) from both ends. Use chain-nose pliers to make a 90° bend at the mark on both pieces. Slide the ½-inch (1.3 cm) coils from step 1 onto the bent wire, positioning them on the 1-inch (2.5 cm) lengths of wire. Slide the second bent 20-gauge wire through both of the tubes to form a rectangle with a coil at each end, with wires extending out each side (figure 1). Anchor wrap a 2½-foot (76.2 cm) piece of 26-gauge wire onto one of the pieces of 20-gauge wire.

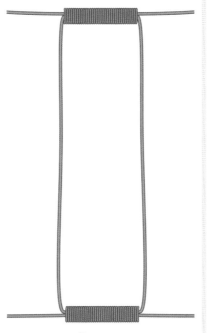

figure 1

SUPPLIES

Silver 18-gauge wire, 3½ feet (1 m)

Silver 20-gauge wire, 9 inches (22.9 cm)

Silver 24-gauge wire, 6 feet (1.8 m)

Silver 26-gauge wire, 62.5 feet (19 m)*

80 jet 2XAB crystal bicones, 3 mm

Midnight blue size 11° round seed beads, 25 g

100 purple pearls, 5 mm

Basic Tool Kit, page 11

Mandrels:

   0.03 inch (0.8 mm)

   0.06 inch (1.6 mm)

   0.04 inch (1 mm)

   0.08 inch (2.1 mm)

*This amount will make a bracelet that fits a 6½-inch (16.5 cm) wrist. Step 4 lists the quantities for other sizes.

FINISHED SIZE

Inner circumference, 6½ inches (16.5 cm)

7 Slide five crystals onto the 26-gauge weaving wire. Begin a two-sided flat weave, with five crystals woven across the front and eight or nine seed beads woven across the back. The first few rows will be a bit awkward, but additional rows will stabilize the weaving and hold the rectangle together firmly. Weave a total of 16 rows, front and back, then wrap twice and trim off any remaining weaving wire. Trim the excess 20-gauge wire that extends from the ends of the coils (figure 2).

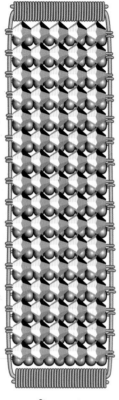

figure 2

Center of the Band

8 Cut two 1-foot (30.5 cm) lengths of 18-gauge wire, and mark them at 5¾ inches (14.6 cm) and at 6 inches (15.2 cm). Cut two 10-inch (25.4 cm) lengths of 18-gauge wire, and mark them at 4¾ inches (12 cm) and at 5 inches (12.7 cm). The longer pieces are the outside wires (OW), and the shorter pieces are the inside wires (IW).

9 Use a two-sided flat weave to begin the center section of the bracelet. Make a bead stop at the end of a 4-foot (1.2 m) piece of 26-gauge wire and string on 7½ inches (19 cm) of seed beads. Anchor wrap the wire around the 5¾-inch (14.6 cm) mark on one OW, slide five seed beads next to the wire, and make one full wrap around the 4¾-inch (12 cm) mark on one IW. Slide five seed beads next to the wire, and make one full wrap around the 4¾-inch (12 cm) mark on the second IW. Slide five seed beads next to the wire, and make one full wrap around the 5¾-inch (14.6 cm) mark on the other OW. Repeat the same pattern across the back. Weave three more rows toward the center marks, front and back, for a total of four rows (figure 3). Trim off the short tail from the beginning.

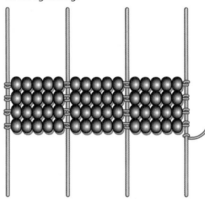

figure 3

Weave the Sides

10 The sides to the left and to the right of the center of the band will be woven the same way, one at a time, with the same number of rows. The number of rows depends on the desired size. Information about the number of rows needed for the desired size of your finished bracelet can be found in step 4.

11 Weave one side using the same wire used to weave the center. The stringing and weaving pattern follows: On the front of row 1 and all odd-numbered rows, string one seed bead and one ¾-inch (1.9 cm) coil. Wrap twice around the first IW. String a coil, wrap twice around the second IW. String a coil and

one seed bead, and wrap once around the OW (figure 4). On the back of all rows, string five seed beads between each of the wires, and make one complete wrap around the outside and inside wires.

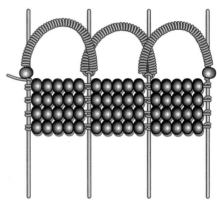

figure 4

12 On even-numbered rows, string one seed bead, one pearl, and one seed bead, and wrap once around the inside and outside wires. Weave the same five-bead pattern used for the odd-numbered rows (figure 5).

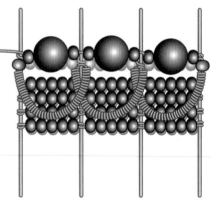

figure 5

13 Add a new wire next to the 5 ¾-inch (14.6 cm) mark, and weave the other side of the bracelet. Use the same pattern described in the previous steps, and weave the same number of rows.

Loop End

14 Weave four rows with five seed beads between each 18-gauge wire on both the front and back. Wrap the weaving wire twice around an outside wire and trim off any remaining wire.

15 Trim the two inside wires ¼ inch (6 mm) past the last wraps. Use round-nose pliers to turn each one into a small loop, rolling the ends toward the bottom of the bracelet, behind the last back row of beads.

16 Slide one of the ¼-inch (6 mm) coils from step 3 onto each of the outside wires. Use chain-nose pliers to make a 90° bend next to each coil, turning the wire toward the center of the bracelet. Slide a ⅞-inch (2.2 cm) coil from step 2 onto one of the wires, and then slide the other wire through the same coil, so the wires pass across each other inside of the coil. Squeeze the sides together, and pull both wire ends to make sure everything is tight. Trim off the ends emerging from the coil (figure 6).

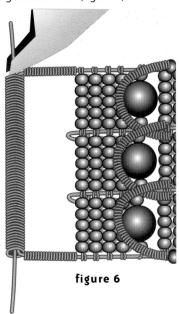

figure 6

Hook End

17 This end is very similar to the other end, except that it needs to be slightly narrower to allow the hook to slide through the loop. Just as on the opposite end, continue to weave if your wire is long enough, or add a new wire if it's shorter than 18 inches (45.7 cm). Weave one row with five seed beads between each 18-gauge wire, then two rows with four seed beads between each wire, and finish by weaving one row with three seed beads between each section. Wrap the weaving wire twice around the nearest outside wire, and trim off any remaining weaving wire.

18 Slide a ¼-inch (6 mm) coil from step 3 onto both of the outside wires. Trim both wires 1 inch (2.5 cm) beyond the ends of the coils, and use chain-nose pliers to bend each wire 90° next to the coil. Slide the ⅝-inch (1.6 cm) coil from step 2 onto one of the wires, then feed the other wire through the coil in the opposite direction. Trim off the wires emerging from the coil. Use chain-nose pliers to grasp about halfway down the side, and pull the end over to form a hook. Bend each side a bit at a time until the hook is fully shaped.

Crystal Band and Final Shaping

19 With the beadwork laid out flat, center the crystal band over the middle of the bracelet. Gently, but firmly, push the sides of the band over the edge of the bracelet until the ends of the band are pushed against the back of the bracelet, next to the weaving.

20 Shape the bracelet on a round object. Clasp the ends and shape the sides into a consistent curve until the bracelet can easily be put on and removed.

> **TIP**
> • Rows will tend to spread apart during weaving. Stop after every few rows and use your fingers and chain-nose pliers to push the rows together. Squeeze with the tips of your pliers to tighten the wraps around the 18-gauge wires.
>
> • Inevitably, you will run out of wire and will need to add a new piece. Always end and add weaving wires around an OW, not an IW.
>
> • Always finish on an even-numbered row.

Silver 20-gauge wire, 5 feet (1.5 meters)

Silver 24-gauge wire, 13 feet (4 meters)

Silver 26-gauge wire, 8 feet (2.5 meters)

Gunmetal size 11° round seed beads, 25 g

Gunmetal size 15° round seed beads, 5 g

100 silver pearls, 3 mm

8 silver pearls, 5 mm

8 hematite AB crystal bicones, 3 mm

1 clear rivoli button, 16 mm

16 head pins, 24 gauge, 1½ inches (3.8 cm)

Basic Tool Kit, page 11

FINISHED SIZE

6½ inches (6.5 cm)

SIZING GUIDE

If you make the 12 rows described in step 2, the resulting bracelet will measure 6½ inches (16.5 cm). To make it longer, for each additional inch (2.5 cm), add four rows on each side of the bracelet. An 8½-inch (21.6 cm) long bracelet, for example, will require 20 rows of weaving.

RAIN FOREST BRACELET

The crystal rivoli at the center represents hidden riches yet to be discovered, with the band symbolizing a broadleaf tree draping its leaves over a river.

Clasp Loop

1 Cut a 4-foot (1.2 m) length of 24-gauge wire. Coil the 24-gauge wire 50 times around a 28-inch (71.1 cm) length of 20-gauge wire, to create a coil about 1 inch (2.5 cm) long. Trim off the short tail at the beginning of the coil. Slide the coil to the center of the 20-gauge wire, and form the wire into a teardrop shape with the wires crossed at the top. Wrap the 24-gauge wire three times around both wires to secure them together.

2 Spread the wires apart to form a V, and wrap the 24-gauge wire once around the 20-gauge wire closest to your body. Begin a two-sided flat weave following the pattern below. P stands for a 3-mm pearl, while all other numbers represent size 11° seed beads.

	Front	Back
Row 1:	1	1
Row 2:	2	2
Row 3:	3	3
Row 4:	4	4
Row 5:	2 P 2	5
Row 6:	6	6
Row 7:	3 P 3	7
Row 8:	8	8
Row 9:	4 P 4	9
Row 10:	10	10
Row 11:	4 P 4	10
Row 12:	10	10
Row 13:	4 P 4	10
Row 14:	10	10

3 If you want a bracelet longer than 6½ inches (16.5 cm), weave the additional desired number of rows for your bracelet size (see Sizing Guide on page 56). The last row should contain only seed beads. Keep track of the number of rows you weave so you can match it when weaving the hook end of the bracelet. Leave the weaving wire in place.

Create the Open Band

4 Cut two 2-inch (5.1 cm) pieces of 20-gauge wire. Use round-nose pliers to make a small loop on one end of each piece.

5 String one size 11° seed bead, one 3-mm pearl, and one 11° seed bead onto the 24-gauge wire weaving wire from the end of the clasp. Position the loop of the 2-inch (5.1 cm) piece of 20-gauge wire next to the last woven row of beads. Hold the wire in place with your non-dominant hand. Wrap from the side to the short piece of 20-gauge wire, wrapping next to the loop. Position

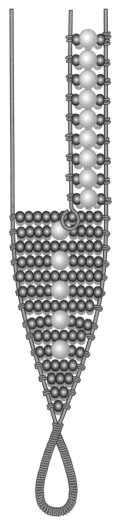

figure 1

the pearl and seed beads next to the previous row of weaving. Continue a two-sided flat weave by weaving three 11° seed beads across the back. Repeat eight more times for a total of nine short rows (figure 1). After weaving the last row, wrap twice around an outer wire, and trim off the remaining wire.

6 Cut a 12-inch (30.5 cm) piece of 24-gauge wire, and anchor wrap it next to the round loop on the second short length of 20-gauge wire. Position it across from the other short length, and hold it in position. String one 11° seed bead, one 3-mm pearl, and one 11° seed bead onto the wire, and wrap across to the outer wire of the bracelet. String three 11° seed beads, and weave back across to the short length of wire. Continue this two-sided flat weave for seven more rows, to match the opposite side. Make two anchor wraps around the short piece of 20-gauge wire and trim off any remaining wire (figure 2).

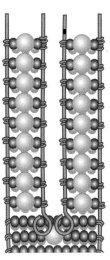

figure 2

7 Cut a 3½-foot (1.1 m) piece of 24-gauge wire. Wrap it twice around one of the outer wires of the band. String one 11° seed bead, one 3-mm pearl, and one 11° seed bead onto the wire. Pull the wire across, and wrap around the nearest short piece of 20-gauge wire. String the same sequence of beads, and wrap across the other short piece of 20-gauge wire. String the sequence one more time, and wrap around the other long piece of 20-gauge wire. Weave back across to the other side, stringing three seed beads between each section of 20-gauge wire (figure 3).

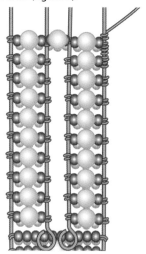

figure 3

8 Measure ⅜ inch (1 cm) from the last wrap on one short piece of 20-gauge wire. Trim off any remaining wire. Use round-nose pliers to form a basic loop with the end. Repeat on the opposite short length of 20-gauge wire.

Pearl Drops and Pearl Spikes

9 The center section of the bracelet features several design elements that need to be prepared before weaving. First, string a bicone and a 5-mm pearl onto a head pin. Make a very small loop, wrap twice, and trim off the rest of the head pin. Repeat seven more times, creating a total of eight pearl drops.

10 Next, make eight pearl spikes as follows. For each, string an 11° seed bead, then a 3-mm pearl onto a head pin, then continue this alternating pattern until there are four seed beads and three pearls on the head pin. Make a very small loop, with two wraps, and trim off the rest of the head pin.

Leaves

11 Cut a 3-inch (7.6 cm) piece of 20-gauge wire. Coil a 12-inch (30.5 cm) piece of 26-gauge wire around the 20-gauge wire 16 times. Cut off the beginning tail. String 30 size 15° seed beads onto the long tail, and make a bead stop at the end of the wire.

12 Slide the 26-gauge coil to the center of the 20-gauge wire and fold the wire in half to form a U. Keep the coil centered on the bend.

13 Begin a two-sided flat weave with a two-bead row. Wrap across the opposite side of the U, and weave a two-bead row behind the previous row. Continue to weave in the following pattern.

Row 2: three beads
Row 3: four beads
Row 4: three beads
Row 5: two beads
Row 6: one bead

14 After completing both sides of the sixth row, wrap twice around the 20-gauge wire, and trim off any remaining 26-gauge wire. Cross one 20-gauge wire over the top of the other. To secure, wrap the top wire once around the bottom wire. Trim off the remaining end of the wrapped wire. Trim the bottom wire to ¼ inch (6 mm) long. Use round-nose

pliers to make a small round loop from the short tail (figure 4).

figure 4

15 Repeat steps 11 to 14 seven more times to make a total of eight leaves.

Decorative Center Leaves

16 Return to working with the band, continuing a two-sided flat weave. Follow the pattern described below for the front rows, and weave 12 size 11° seed beads across the back for all rows. Keep the weaving taut and snug, especially on rows containing spikes, leaves, and other movable elements.

Row 1: 11° seed bead, 5-mm pearl, two 11° seed beads, pearl drop, two 11° seed beads, 5-mm pearl, 11° seed bead
Row 2: 11° seed bead, 3-mm pearl, two 11° seed beads, 3-mm pearl, two 11° seed beads, 3-mm pearl, 11° seed bead
Row 3: 11° seed bead, pearl spike, 11° seed bead, leaf, 11° seed bead, 5-mm pearl, 11° seed bead, leaf, 11° seed bead, pearl spike, 11° seed bead
Row 4: 11° seed bead, 3-mm pearl, two 11° seed beads, 3-mm pearl, two 11° seed beads, 3-mm pearl, 11° seed bead
Row 5: 11° seed bead, pearl spike, 11° seed bead, leaf, 11° seed bead, 3-mm pearl, two 11° seed beads, 3-mm pearl, 11° seed bead
Row 6: five 11° seed beads, rivoli button, five 11° seed beads.

17 Weave 12 size 11° seed beads across the back to complete the sixth row (figure 5). After weaving row 6, weave in reverse: row 5, then 4, 3, 2 and 1. The rivoli button should be in the center of this section of the bracelet, encircled by leaves and pearl spikes. Wrap the weaving wire twice around the 20-gauge wire and trim any remaining wire.

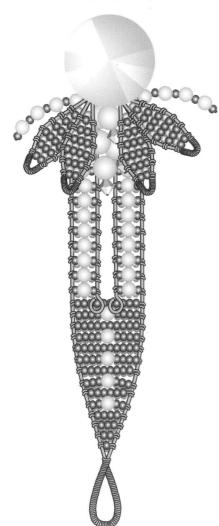

figure 5

Second Half of Band

18 Repeat steps 4 through 6.

19 After completing the open rows, weave the same number of rows you completed in step 3, but in reverse, starting with a seed bead row, both front and back.

20 After weaving all the way back to a single seed bead row, wrap twice around the crossed 20-gauge wires and trim off the remaining weaving wire. Grasp one 20-gauge wire, wrap it twice around the other wire, and trim the wrapped wire close to the remaining 20-gauge wire. Don't cut the 20-gauge wire; you'll use it in the next step.

Clasp Hook

21 Wrap a 1½-foot (45.7 cm) piece of 24-gauge wire 75 times around the remaining 20-gauge wire to form a coil about 1½ inches (3.8 cm) long. Trim off both ends of the 24-gauge wire. Position the coil 1/16 inch (1.6 mm) from the 20-gauge wraps. Pinch the coil and wire in half, until the ends of the coil line up (figure 6).

figure 6

22 Use chain-nose pliers to hold the wires steady, next to each other. Wrap the 20-gauge wire twice between the ends of the coil and the previous 20-gauge wraps, and trim off the remaining wire. Use round-nose pliers to form the doubled ends into a hook, which should overlap the wrapped 20-gauge wire at the base of the hook.

23 Use chain-nose pliers to open one of the 20-gauge loops located at the ends of the open band. Slide a pearl drop into the loop and use the pliers to close it again. Add one dangle to the other three loops in the same position.

Variation

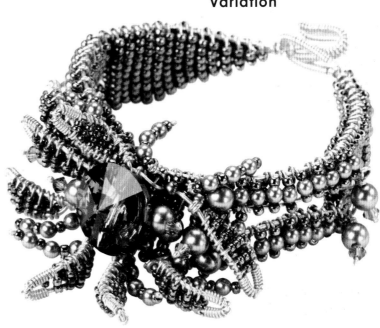

ENCHANTED BRACELET

Coiled corkscrews, curvaceous fan-like shapes, and flirtatious pearl clusters turn a simple bracelet into a wearable sculptural wonder. Seed beads provide color and texture, and set the mood for the entire bracelet.

SIZING GUIDE

The bead counts and measurements given in the instructions make a bracelet 6¾ inches (17.1 cm) long.

• To make a bracelet 7½ inches (19 cm) long, string 98 seed beads, and add two rows to the weaving, for a total of 13 rows. The widest row of the woven portion will be comprised of seven beads.

• For a bracelet 8¼ inches (21 cm) long, string 128 seed beads, and add four rows to the weaving, for a total of 15 rows. The widest row will be comprised of eight beads.

• To create a bracelet 8¾ inches (22.2 cm) long, string 158 beads, and add six rows to the weaving, for a total of 17 rows. The widest row will be comprised of nine beads.

Clasp Loop

1 Cut 4 feet (1.2 m) of 24-gauge wire and make careful side-by-side wraps around the mandrel to produce a coil 4 inches (10.2 cm) long. Cut this coil into four separate 1-inch (2.5 cm) coils.

2 Cut a 3-foot (1.5 m) length of 24-gauge wire. Coil it 50 times around a 30-inch (76.2 cm) piece of 20-gauge wire, until the coil is about 1 inch (2.5 cm) long. Trim off the short tail at the beginning of the coil. Slide the coil to the center of the 20-gauge wire, and form the wire into a teardrop shape with the wires crossed at the top. Wrap the 24-gauge wire three times around both wires to secure them.

3 Coil the 24-gauge wire 50 more times around one of the pieces of 20-gauge wire, creating a coil about 1 inch (2.5 cm) long. Hold the coil in position, and wrap the coiled section loosely around the other 20-gauge wire. Create two full, loose wraps (figure 1). Wrap the weaving wire twice around both wires.

figure 1

Half of the Fans

4 Separate the two 20-gauge wires to form a V. Wrap once around the wire nearest to your body. For a bracelet 6¾-inches (17.1 cm) long, string 72 seed beads onto the 24-gauge wire—or use the sizing guide to determine how many beads you need to string to a bracelet in your desired size—then make a bead stop on the end of the wire.

5 Begin a two-sided flat weave. As you weave the rows, form the 20-gauge wire into a curved shape. Weave a total of 11 rows, front and back. Start with a single bead row, and make each row one bead longer until you've woven both sides of a six-bead row. As you weave, develop and refine the curve of the 20-gauge wire. After weaving the sixth row, make each row one bead shorter until you taper back down to a single bead row (front and back), as shown in figure 2.

figure 2

6 After completing the single bead rows, wrap the weaving wire twice around the 20-gauge wire, then trim off any excess wire. Slide one of the 1-inch (2.5 cm) coils completed in step 1 onto the wire at the end of the woven section. Hold the coil snug against the previous wraps, and wrap the coil-encased 20-gauge wire twice, loosely, around the other 20-gauge wire, trying to match the coiled wraps at the base of the clasp loop.

7 Anchor wrap an 18-inch (45.7 cm) length of 24-gauge wire around the 20-gauge wire coming straight through the coiled wraps.

8 Repeat steps 4, 5, and 6 until you've completed five fans. After adding the coiled wraps, wrap the bare 20-gauge wire twice around the other piece of 20-gauge wire. Trim off the remaining

SUPPLIES

Silver 20-gauge wire, 5 feet (1.5 m)

Silver 24-gauge wire, 21 feet (6.5 m)

Metallic purple iris size 15° round seed beads, 25 g

50 purple pearls, 5 mm

42 head pins, 24 gauge, 1½ inches (3.5 cm)*

Basic Tool Kit, page 11

0.03-inch (0.08 mm) mandrel

*Or an additional 6¼ feet (2 m) of silver 24-gauge wire if you want to make your own head pins

FINISHED SIZE

6¾ inches (17.1 cm)

wire from the wrapping half only. Leave one wire intact, coming straight out of the end of the bracelet (figure 3; a portion of the drawing has been cropped out to fit on page).

figure 3

Clasp Hook

9 Wrap an 18-inch (45.7 cm) piece of 24-gauge wire 75 times around the remaining piece of 20-gauge wire, creating a coil 1½ inches (3.8 cm) long. Trim off both ends of the 24-gauge wire.

10 Leave a ⅛-inch (3 mm) gap between the coil and the last wraps. Use chain-nose pliers to fold the coil at the center. Hold both wires in the jaws of your chain-nose pliers, next to the ends of the coils. Wrap the 20-gauge wire twice at the base of the hook, and trim off the remaining wire. Use round-nose pliers to bend the doubled wires into a hook.

Remaining Fans

11 The second side of the bracelet consists of fans only, with no clasp or coiled wraps to worry about. Cut two 13-inch (33 cm) lengths of 20-gauge wire. Mark both wires 1 inch (2.5 cm) from one end.

12 Cut an 18-inch (45.7 cm) piece of 24-gauge wire. String the same number of beads as you did in step 4, then make a bead stop at the end of the wire.

13 Line up the marks on the two pieces of 20-gauge wire and wrap the 24-gauge wire three times around the marks. Repeat step 5 to complete the first fan of the second half of the bracelet. After completing the single bead rows, wrap the 24-gauge wire twice and trim off any remaining wire. Unwrap two of the wraps from the starting end of the weaving wire, and trim off any remaining wire.

14 Wrap one of the 20-gauge wires twice around the other wire, trim off the wrapped end, and leave the other wire intact.

15 Slide the long ends of the 20-gauge wires through the second set of wrapped coils on the first half of the bracelet. Slide the short ends of the 20-gauge wires through the first set of coils. The fan should fit snugly between the wrapped coils, and curve in the direction opposite the first fan (figure 4).

figure 4

16 Cut the single, short 20-gauge wire coming out of the wrapped coils to ½ inch (1.3 cm) long. Use round-nose pliers to form the short wire into a simple round loop (figure 5).

figure 5

17 Finish the second side by weaving four more fans. Each time, start with an 18-inch (45.7 cm) piece of weaving wire, string the beads, anchor wrap the wire onto the 20-gauge wire, weave the rows, and trim off the excess weaving wire. After adding each fan, slide the two pieces of 20-gauge wire through the next wrapped coil, and continue. After adding the last fan, repeat step 14. Feed the remaining piece of 20-gauge wire through the last wrapped coil, and repeat step 16 (figure 6; a portion of the drawing has been cropped out to fit on page).

Pearl Clusters

If, instead of using commercial head pins for this project, you prefer to make them yourself, cut 42 pieces of 24-gauge wire, each 1¾ inches (4.4 cm) long, and follow the instructions on page 25.

18 To make a pearl dangle, string one seed bead and one pearl on a head pin. Make a wrapped loop above the beads. Keep the loop as small as possible, and only wrap once or twice before trimming off the wire ends. Repeat to make a total of 42 pearl dangles.

19 Make three small loops at the end of a 1½-inch (3.8 cm) piece of 20-gauge wire, using the same technique as if you were making a bead stop. String one pearl and five pearl dangles, and feed the wire through the second set of coiled wraps. String on five pearl dangles, and one pearl. Make three small loops at the end of the wire. If the wire is still loose, and is wrapped more than three times, carefully trim off any extra loops, and ensure that tension keeps the elements tightly clustered. Add identical clusters to each of the other three coiled wraps in the middle of the bracelet.

20 Add one of the remaining two dangles to the simple 20-gauge wire loops finished in steps 16 and 17.

Variation

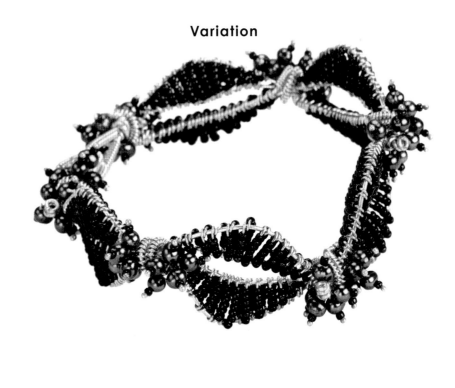

figure 6

SUPPLIES

Silver 16-gauge wire, 6 feet (1.2 m)

Silver 20-gauge wire, 18 inches (46 cm)

Silver 26-gauge wire, 16 feet (5.8 m)

Metallic burgundy size 11° round seed beads, 5 g

Basic Tool Kit, page 11

Mandrels:

½ inch (1.3 cm)

¾ inch (1.9 cm)

0.03 inch (0.8 mm)

0.05 inch (1.3 mm)

Micro torch

FINISHED SIZE

7¼ inches (18.9 cm) long

CIRCLES BRACELET

Soldered rings form the basis for a sinuous woven structure. The design plays with geometric shapes, negative and positive spaces, and interlocking curves.

Woven Circles

1 Cut three 2½-inch (6.4 cm) and three 1¾-inch (4.4 cm) pieces of 16-gauge wire. Shape three large rings around the mandrel with a ¾-inch (1.9 cm) diameter, and three small rings around the mandrel with a ½-inch (1.3 cm) diameter, then solder them all (page 26).

2 Cut 21 inches (53.3 cm) of 26-gauge wire. Make a bead stop at one end of the wire, and string on 15 seed beads. Anchor wrap this around one of the small soldered rings. Place the small ring inside of a large ring, hold the seed bead between the two rings, and make one full wrap around the large ring. Weave back across to the small ring, leaving an exposed wire between the two rings, and begin a single-sided flat weave. Position the rings close together when you begin the weave. As you weave the second half of the ring, allow a larger gap to form between the two rings.

3 Continue until all 15 beads are woven between the rings. String and individually weave on five more rows of single beads. After adding the 20th bead, wrap twice and trim off any remaining wire (figure 1). Repeat steps 2 and 3 with the other two pairs of rings made in step 1.

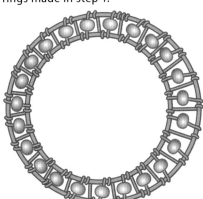

figure 1

Prepare the Coils

4 Coil 1½ feet (45.7 cm) of 20-gauge wire around the 0.03-inch (0.8 mm) mandrel. Cut the coil into two pieces, each 7/16 inch (1.1 cm) long. Coil 3 feet (91.4 cm) of 26-gauge wire around the 0.05-inch (1.3 mm) mandrel. Cut one length of coil to 7/8 inches (2.2 cm), and one to 1⅜ inches (3.5 cm).

Band Front

5 Cut two 12-inch (30.5 cm) pieces of 16-gauge wire. Mark each piece 3½ inches (8.9 cm) from one end. Anchor wrap a piece of 26-gauge wire 4 feet (1.2 m) long onto the outer ring of one woven circle. Align the wraps on the circle with the mark, and wrap once around one piece of 16-gauge wire.

6 The circle is woven with a variation of a single-sided flat weave, as follows. String one seed bead. Align the 3 ½-inch (8.9 cm) marks, and make one complete wrap around the second 16-gauge wire (figure 2). Cross back to the first 16-gauge wire, leaving an exposed wire across the back, and wrap once around the wire. Weave clockwise, bringing the wire underneath the woven circle, and back up between the first row of beads

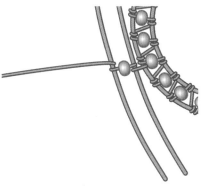

figure 2

(figure 3). One row is now complete, and the wire is positioned to begin the second row. String a seed bead, pull the wire across, and make a complete wrap around the outer 16-gauge wire of the band. Continue across the back of the band wires, across to the circle, and back to the front, making each row at least 1/16 inch (1.6 mm) apart from the previous one, and attaching it to the circle between each row of beads.

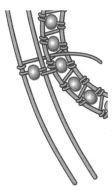

figure 3

7 Shape the 16-gauge wires around the woven circle. Weave 10 rows, then string on the bead for the 11th row, wrap around the outer 16-gauge wire, and wrap down between two rows of a second woven circle. Weave underneath the back of the circle, returning to the outer 16-gauge wire of the band, which is now the inner 16-gauge wire of the band for the second circle. String one seed bead, and weave across to the other 16-gauge wire in the band.

8 Continue to weave counterclockwise, and add 10 rows. Add another seed bead, weave across between two rows of the third woven circle, and then back up through the circle to the front, as in step 6, to complete row 11. Weave 11 more clockwise rows, and shape the two 16-gauge wires around the third circle. After row 11, wrap the wire twice and trim off any remaining weaving wire (figure 4).

Band Sides

9 Position the two end curves of the band upward. Shape the 16-gauge wires so they straighten out horizontally from the circles (figure 5).

figure 5

10 Anchor wrap a piece of 26-gauge wire 3½ feet (1 m) long around the third woven circle. Trim off the short tail. Begin a two-sided flat weave with a single-bead row. Weave two beads on each side of rows 2 and 3. Add one bead to each of the next four rows until row 7, which is six beads wide, is complete. Repeat on the opposite side of the bead-work (figure 6).

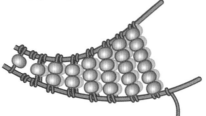

figure 6

11 The bead counts and measurements given in the instructions make a bracelet 7¼ inches (18.9 cm) long. To make your bracelet a different size, see the sizing guide below to determine the number of decorative rows needed for the proper length. Cut two pieces of 16-gauge wire, each 2½ inches (6.4 cm) long. Position one wire next to the last wraps after row 7, to sit inside of the side of the 16-gauge frame. Hold the wire in position, pull the wire across, come up between the two 16-gauge wires, and make one complete the wrap around the inner wire (figure 7).

figure 7

SIZING GUIDE

- To make a bracelet 6½ inches (16.5 cm) long, weave seven decorative rows, and then mark ⅝ inch (1.6 cm) from the last row.

- For a bracelet 7¾ inches (19.7 cm) long, weave 10 to 12 decorative rows, and then mark ⅞ inch (2.2 cm) from the last row.

- For a bracelet 8¼ inches (21 cm) long, weave 14 decorative rows, then mark 1 inch (2.5 cm) from the last row.

- For larger sizes, add between two and four rows for each additional ½ inch (1.3 cm) needed, and mark 1⅛ inch (2.8 cm) from the last row.

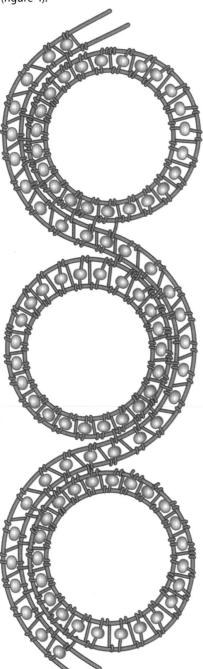

figure 4

12 String four seed beads. Position and hold the second new wire on the inside of the opposite side of the frame. Pull the weaving wire across the bracelet, wrap once around the new wire, pull the wire across both wires toward the outside, come up between the two wires, and complete one full wrap around the outer wire (figure 8). Wrap once around the inside wire, string four seed beads, pull the wire across, wrap around the inner wire, and continue the same sequence of wraps used for the front half of the row. This slight variation of a two-sided flat weave accommodates the two extra wires.

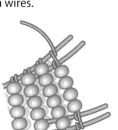

figure 8

13 Repeat the previous step five more times for a total of six decorative rows (for a bracelet 7¼ inches [18.4 cm] long). Mark the outer wire ¾ inch (1.9 cm) from the last decorative row. Refer to the sizing guide to verify the measurements and number of rows needed for your size. Mark the inner wire ⅛ inch (3 mm) shorter than the outer wire. Trim each inner wire at the mark. Use chain-nose pliers to bend the outer wires 90° toward the center. Trim both outer wires ³⁄₁₆ inch (5 mm) from the 90° bend. Slide both of the ends into one of the 20-gauge coils from step 4. Push the sides together to trap the coil in place.

14 After completing the last decorative row, weave four seven-bead rows, front and back, between the two outside wires, until the weaving is next to the end coil (figure 9).

figure 9

Clasp Loop

15 Cut a 2⅜-inch (5.4 cm) piece of 16-gauge wire. From each end, mark the wire at ⅝ inch (1.6 mm) and ¾ inch (1.9 cm). Slide the ⅞-inch (2.2 cm) coil from step 4 to the center of the wire. Shape the coil into a curve. Use chain-nose pliers to make 90° inward bends at the ⅝-inch (1.6 cm) marks. Slide each end through the 20-gauge tube at one end of the bracelet. Push the sides together, and trim each wire as it emerges from the coil.

Clasp Hook

16 Cut a 3⅛-inch (8 cm) piece of 16-gauge wire. From each end, mark the wire at ⅝ inch (1.6 mm) and ⅞ inch (2.2 cm). Slide the 1⅜-inch (3.5 cm) coil from step 4 to the center of the wire, between the ⅞-inch (2.2 cm) marks. Shape the coil into a curve, and then use chain-nose pliers to squeeze it until it's narrow enough to slide through the loop. Bend each wire 90° inward at the ⅞-inch (2.2 cm) marks. Insert the ends through the end coil. Push the sides inward, and trim the wires where they emerge from the coil. Use round-nose pliers to bend the hook in the middle and double it back over itself. Adjust the width of the hook as needed until it slides in and out of the loop easily.

Variation

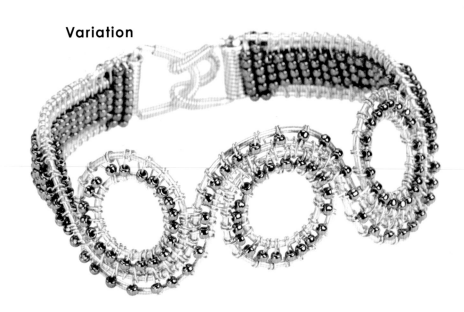

Pendants

A pendant is the perfect vehicle for showing off a spectacular focal bead.

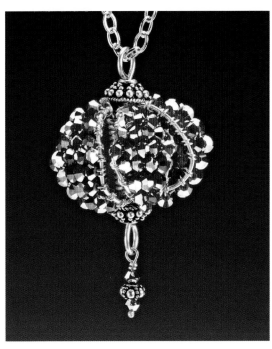

SUPPLIES

Silver 20-gauge wire, 3 feet (90.5 cm)

Silver 26-gauge wire, 9 feet (2.8 m)

Burgundy metallic size 15° seed beads, 3 g

One round cabochon, 1³⁄₈ inch (3.5 cm) diameter

Basic Tool Kit, page 11

FINISHED SIZE

1½ inches (3.8 cm) in diameter

TIP

All rows of this bezel are beaded. Each loop sits ¹⁄₁₆ inch (1.6 mm) from the previous one, to make a space that fits a single size 15° seed bead.

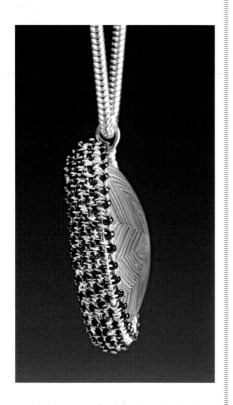

ENTRAPPED ELEGANCE PENDANT

Capture and enhance the cabochon of your choice with a bead and wire bezel. This versatile technique can be used for nearly any round or oval stone, found object, glass cabochon, or crystal stone.

1 Cut a piece of 20-gauge wire 3 feet (90.5 cm) long. This is enough wire to make a bezel for a cabochon measuring between 1 and 2½ inches (2.5–6.4 cm) in diameter, with a depth of ¼ to 5/16 inches (6–8 mm). **Note:** If your cabochon is larger than that, measure its circumference. Multiply that amount by eight, and add 2 inches (5.1 cm) to the total.

2 Mark the wire 1 inch (2.5 cm) from the end. Anchor wrap a 3-foot (91.4 cm) piece of 26-gauge wire around the mark. Shape a few loops around the cabochon, or an object that is roughly the same shape and size.

3 Referring to the Bezel Weave instructions starting on page 20, weave the first loop of the bezel with size 15° seed beads. Check the fit; the loop should overlap 1/16 inch (1.6 mm) over the front of the cabochon. Tighten or loosen the loop as needed, and then continue to weave the second loop.

4 The second loop of the bezel will form the side. To begin the second row of the bezel, feed the weaving wire up between the first and second loops, between the first and second beads of the first loop. This begins the third loop. String a single size 15° seed bead, and make one complete wrap around the third loop (figure 1). Bring the wire back

up through the second and third loops, between the second and third beads of the first loop, and string another size 15° seed bead. Make one complete wrap around the third loop (figure 2). Continue to weave in this manner until two rows are complete.

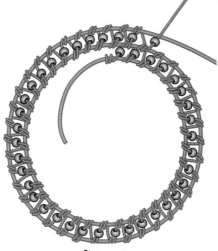

figure 2

5 Weave as many more rows as needed to encase the sides of the cabochon. As you form the bezel, check it frequently to make sure it maintains the correct contour and size. Continue to shape the 20-gauge wire as you weave.

6 After the sides are woven, begin to weave a row that will overlap the back edge of the cabochon by 1/16 inch (1.6 mm). Weave the first three bead rows in place, and insert the cabochon into the bezel. Weave around the loop until the weaving lines up with the 20-gauge tail wire on the front of the cabochon. Weave seven more rows. Wrap the weaving wire twice around the 20-gauge wire, and trim off any remaining wire.

7 Trim the 20-gauge wire in the back to 1 inch (2.5 cm), and form this end into a spiral. On the front, trim the 20-gauge wire tail to 3/8 inch (1 cm). Use round-nose pliers to roll the wire back, and form a round loop.

Variation

figure 1

SUPPLIES

Silver 18-gauge wire, 1 foot (30.5 cm)

Silver 20-gauge wire, 4 feet (1.2 m)

Silver 24-gauge half-hard wire, 4 feet (1.2 m for head pins only)

Silver 24-gauge soft wire, 12 feet (3.5 m)

20 to 30 dorado bicones, 3 mm

21 bronze pearls, 5 mm

1 lampworked focal bead, 22–28 mm

Size 11° seed beads:

  Silver, 3g

  Bronze, 3 g

Basic Tool Kit, page 11

5/32-inch center punch

0.04-inch (1 mm) mandrel

Micro torch

FINISHED SIZE

3½ inches (8.9 cm)

SATURN PENDANT

The pendant has a marvelous spiral shape that hints at a far-off place in the universe. When worn, this cosmic manifestation will attract interest, attention, and compliments.

Core and Spray

1 Start by making head pins, as follows. Cut sixteen 3-inch (7.6 cm) pieces of 24-gauge half-hard wire, and follow the instructions on page 25. Then string one bicone and one pearl on each head pin. These head pins will eventually form the spray at the bottom of the pendant. Set them aside.

2 Wrap a 12-inch (30.5 cm) length of 18-gauge wire around the center punch, starting at the largest diameter on the punch and forming a coiled cone (figure 1). Slide the cone off of the punch and trim the ends flush.

figure 1

3 Coil 26 inches (66 cm) of 24-gauge soft wire around the mandrel, making a 3-inch (7.6 cm) coil.

4 Cut a 9-inch (22.9 cm) piece of 20-gauge wire. Slide the 3-inch (7.6 cm) coil to the center of the 9-inch (22.9 cm) piece of wire. With the coil in position, fold the wire in half. It will now be described as two wires in these instructions.

5 Slide the lampworked bead onto the folded 20-gauge wires. Next, slide the cone onto the two wires with the small end positioned next to the bead.

6 Arrange the head pins into a pleasing configuration, making a cluster to place at the bottom of the pendant. Hold this spray in front of the two pieces of 20-gauge wire and the cone, with the ends of the head pins pointing up toward the lampworked bead. Leave ½ inch (1.3 cm) or more between the bottom of the cone and the tops of the beads on the head pins.

7 When you're satisfied with the arrangement, wrap a 5-inch (12.7 cm) piece of 24-gauge soft wire around the bundle of head pins and the two 20-gauge wires coming out of the bead. Begin to fold the 24-gauge wires down over the wrapped wire (figure 2). Once all head pins are folded over, cut the head pin wires to about ¼ inch (6 mm). Use chain-nose

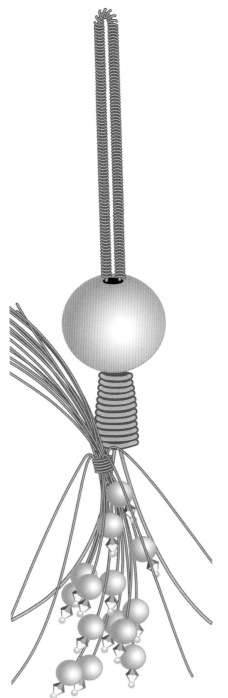

figure 2

pliers to mash and compress the bundled wires until the cone slides down and covers them completely.

8 Fold the remaining 20-gauge wire ends up over the sides of the cone (figure 3). Leave ½ inch (1.3 cm), and trim off any remaining wire. Repeat with the other wire. Bend, twist, and push the ends up into the cone until they can't be seen.

figure 3

Spiral Element

9 Cut a 7-foot (2.1 m) piece of 24-gauge soft wire. Coil the 24-gauge wire 30 times around a 20-inch (50.8 cm) piece 20-gauge wire. Measure 8 inches (20.3 cm) from one end of the 20-gauge wire. Make a 90° bend. The longer half is the outer wire, the shorter half is the inner wire. Slide the coil to the center, fold it in the middle, and position the long end of the 24-gauge weaving wire on the short (inner) half of the wire.

10 Begin a two-sided flat weave. String three seed beads of any color. Lay the beads between the 20-gauge wires and wrap around the outer wire. String three more seed beads—again, any color—and cross back to the starting side, completing the first row, front and back, of the weave. There is no set pattern for this weave; it's improvisational, and can include crystals or pearls in addition to multiple colors of seed beads, inspired by the palette of the focal bead.

11 While continuing to weave rows, curve the 20-gauge wire frame wires around the side of the lampworked bead so as to wrap it around the bead. Slide the

doubled center down over the 20-gauge wires coming out of the top of the bead. As the weave becomes longer, spread the two 20-gauge wires apart by making the rows wider, and form a slight fan shape that reaches its widest point toward the bottom of the focal bead (figure 4). The widest rows should contain five to seven seed beads.

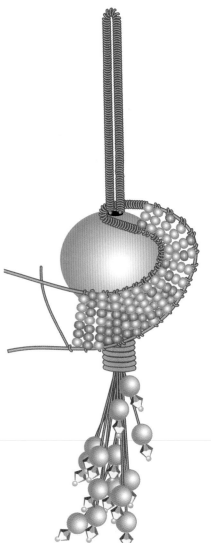

figure 4

12 After achieving a pleasing shape and weaving multiple longer rows, taper the weave back down to rows three seed beads wide. Weave 10 to 12 rows of the same width, front and back. Add one last row, single sided, weaving a 4-mm pearl between the 20-gauge wires. Make two wraps on the outer wire and trim off the excess 24-gauge weaving wire (figure 5).

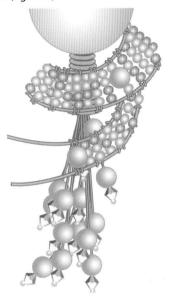

figure 5

Hook

13 Trim the 20-gauge ends to ⅜ inch (1 cm). Use round-nose pliers to form the ends into loops. Above the lampworked bead, use round-nose pliers to form the doubled wires into a hook (figure 6).

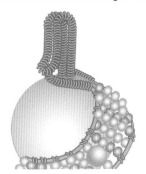

figure 6

Variation

CROWN JEWEL PENDANT

Five crystal-encrusted crescents form a modern interpretation of an elaborate and regal orb.

1 Coil 12 inches (30.5 cm) of 18-gauge wire around the mandrel. Trim the coil to ½ inch (13 mm). Cut 10 lengths of 20-gauge wire, each 3 inches (7.6 cm) long. Mark each of these 1 inch (2.5 cm) from one end. Cut five pieces of 26-gauge wire, each 14 inches (35.6 cm) long.

2 Wrap a 14-inch (35.6 cm) piece of 26-gauge wire twice around the 1-inch mark of two pieces of 20-gauge wire. These are temporary wraps that will be removed later. Spread the two wires apart to form a V. Wrap once around the wire closest to your body.

3 Begin a two-sided flat weave. Weave the first six rows, then bend the wire at a 45° angle, back toward the middle, to form a diamond. Keep the rows snug so the crystals nest next to one another. Weave the following pattern (SB stands for seed bead, and B for bicone).

Row	Front	Back
1	1 SB	1 SB
2	1 B	2 SB
3	2 B	4 SB
4	3 B	5 SB
5	4 B	6 SB
6	5B	7 SB
7	4 B	6 SB
8	3 B	5 SB
9	2 B	3 SB
10	1 B	1 SB
11	1 SB	—

4 On the last row, no beads are woven across the back. Wrap twice around the 20-gauge wire, and cut off the remaining wire. Unwrap two wraps from the beginning of the weave, and cut off the remaining weaving wire (figure 1).

figure 1

5 Repeat steps 2, 3, and 4 four more times to create a total of five diamond shapes.

6 Shape each of the diamonds into a crescent by wrapping it around a fine-point marker. Be sure to bend the beadwork as uniformly as possible.

7 Using chain-nose pliers, grasp the two wires at the bottom of one crescent. Bend the wires across the curve, parallel to the coil in the center. Trim the wires ¼ inch (6 mm) from the bend. Repeat with the other pair of wires (figure 2). Repeat with the four remaining diamonds.

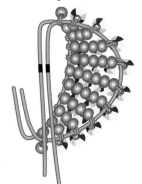

figure 2

8 Push the ends of three of the crescents into the coil and squeeze each crescent to adjust the shape (figure 3).

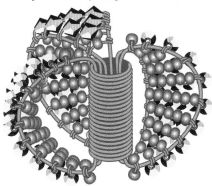

figure 3

9 Insert the remaining two crescents into the coil. Reshape all of the crescents to form a pleasing spherical shape. You may need to use chain-nose pliers to pull and push the ends of the last crescent into position.

10 Use round-nose pliers to form a simple loop on one end of a 3-inch (7.6 cm) piece of 18-gauge wire. String a bead cap onto the wire, and insert it through the coil. String a bead cap onto the other end of the wire, and form a second loop. Make sure that all elements are in position, and that the loop holds everything tightly.

11 Form a wrapped dangle with one bicone, the Bali silver bead, and another bicone, and attach it to the bottom loop.

Variation

Silver 16-gauge wire, 6 inches
(15.2 cm)

Silver 20-gauge wire, 2 feet (61 cm)

Silver 26-gauge wire, 13 feet (3.7 m)

Burgundy metallic size
15° seed beads, 4 g

20 volcano orange crystal sequins,
3 mm

20 light green crystal pearls, 5 mm

1 lampworked bead, 14 mm with
large hole

1 Bali silver bead cap, 8 mm

20 silver head pins, 24 gauge,
1½ inches (3.8 cm)

Basic Tool kit, page 11

0.05-inch (1.3 mm) mandrel

Micro torch

FINISHED SIZE

3¼ inches (8.3 cm)

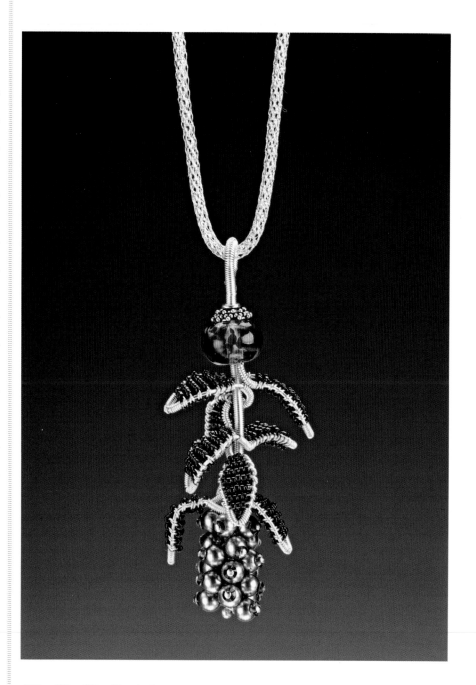

FORBIDDEN FRUIT
PENDANT

**This seductive pendant gathers leaves and pearls into an orderly yet
organically shaped cluster.**

Weave the Leaves

1 Make a mark 3 inches (7.6 cm) from the end of the 2-foot (61 cm) piece of 20-gauge wire. This will be the center of a leaf. Mark the wire ¾ inch (1.9 cm) from the center mark, on both sides.

2 Make a bead stop on the end of a 13-inch (33-cm) piece of 26-gauge wire. String 64 size 15° seed beads onto the wire. Wrap the wire 15 times around the marked piece of 20-gauge wire, cut off the short tail, and center the coil on the 3-inch (7.6 cm) mark.

3 Bend the 20-gauge wire and coil at the 3-inch (7.6 cm) mark, and line up the ¾-inch (1.9 cm) marks on each side (figure 1). Use chain-nose pliers to squeeze the coil and wire to create a slight point at the center.

figure 1

4 Begin a two-sided flat weave, starting with a three-bead row on both the front and back. Weave three more rows, and add one bead to each row, for a total of four rows, with the fourth containing six beads (figure 2). Use chain-nose pliers to bend the 20-gauge wire to form a diamond shape.

figure 2

5 Weave four more rows, with each row one bead narrower than the previous one, for a total of eight completed rows. The final row will be two beads wide, front and back. After the eighth row is complete, wrap the weaving wire 12 times around the 20-gauge wire and trim off any remaining weaving wire (figure 3).

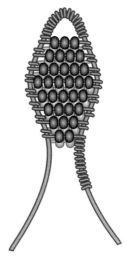

figure 3

Variation

6 Use chain-nose pliers to bend both wires at the base of the eighth row 90°, facing in opposite directions (figure 4). Make one mark ¾ inch (1.9 cm) from the end of the coil, and a second mark 1½ inches (3.8 cm) from the end of the coil.

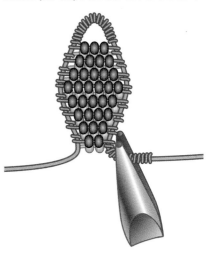

figure 4

7 Make a bead stop on the end of a 13-inch (33 cm) piece of 26-gauge wire. String 64 seed beads onto the wire. Wrap the wire 15 times around the marked piece of 20-gauge wire, cut off the short tail, and center the tube on the first ¾-inch (1.9 cm) mark.

8 Repeat steps 4 through 6 to complete a second leaf.

9 Weave a total of nine leaves in a long row (figure 5).

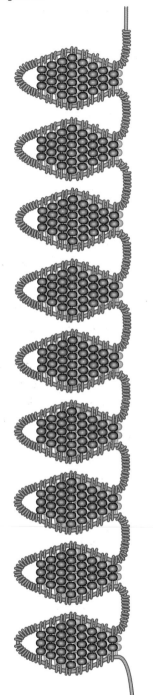

figure 5

Assemble the Cluster

10 Coil 3 feet (91.4 cm) of 26-gauge wire around the mandrel to make a coil 2½ inches (6.4 cm) long. Trim two separate coils, one 1¼ inches (3.2 cm), and a second 1 inch (2.5 cm) long. Set aside.

11 Follow the instructions on page 25 to create a head pin from a 6-inch (15.2 cm) piece of 16-gauge wire.

12 Prepare 20 dangles, each one consisting of a 3-mm crystal sequin and a 5-mm pearl strung on a head pin, and closed with a wire-wrapped loop large enough to fit on the 16-gauge wire.

13 String all 20 dangles onto the head pin. Wrap the 3-inch (7.6 cm) end of the 20-gauge wire with the woven leaves three times around the head pin, and trim off the short tail.

14 String the 1¼-inch (3.2 cm) coil from step 10 onto the 16-gauge wire. Slide all the elements down to the bottom of the head pin (figure 6). Wrap the 20-gauge wire four times around the head pin. The wraps should be near the head pin without touching it. Shape the end of each leaf, from center to tip, so it points down.

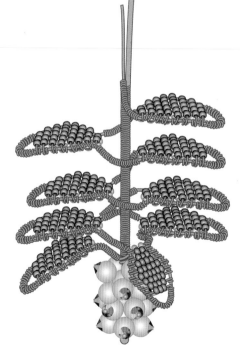

figure 6

15 Slide the lampworked bead over both the head pin and the 20-gauge wire, push all the elements down to the bottom of the head pin, and arrange all the leaves to achieve a pleasing shape. Wrap the 20-gauge wire twice around the head pin, and trim off any remaining 20-gauge wire. Slide the bead cap onto the head pin, and push it down to hide the wraps above the bead (figure 7). Slide the 1-inch (2.5 cm) coil made in step 10 onto the head pin, and push it snug against the bead cap.

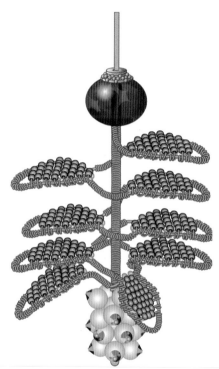

figure 7

16 Make a mark on the 16-gauge wire, ¼ inch (6 mm) from the end of the coil. Use a chasing hammer to flatten and spread this marked end into a paddle. Use round-nose pliers to form the paddle into a small loop. Use the widest point on the round-nose pliers to shape the 1-inch (2.5 cm) section into a hook.

DE ROS PENDANT

While exploring my family tree, I discovered a link to the De Ros family, a European clan of royal heritage. This unique pendant is designed as a wearable family crest.

DALLAS LEVETT'S WOVEN BEAD & WIRE JEWELRY **81**

SUPPLIES

Silver 20-gauge wire, 1 foot (30.5 cm)

Silver 26-gauge wire, 19 feet (5.8 m)

Transparent pink green iris size 11° round seed beads, 5 g

1 volcano crystal button, 10 mm

Basic Tool Kit, page 11

0.03-inch (0.8 mm) mandrel

FINISHED SIZE

1½ inches (3.8 cm) in diameter

Weave the Beaded Center

1 Mark the 1-foot (30.5 cm) piece of 20-gauge wire 2 inches (5.1 cm) from one end. Use chain-nose pliers to make a 90° bend at the mark. Use round-nose pliers to form a clockwise loop above the bend with the long end of the wire (figure 1). Make a loop roughly ⁵⁄₁₆-inch (8 mm) in diameter, so when the button is set on top of the loop later, its edge will overlap the wire.

figure 1

2 Position the tail wire of a 2½-foot (76.2 cm) piece of 26-gauge wire next to the 90° bend and anchor wrap around the 20-gauge wire with the tail positioned next to the 90° bend. Cut off the short tail and slide the wraps as close as possible to the bend.

3 Begin a two-sided flat weave. Weave one bead, and position it in the V formed where the 20-gauge wire overlaps. Weave a single bead on the back of the first row (figure 2). For the second row, string two beads. As you weave, use your fingers to curve the wire into an even circle. Weave 14 more rows until you've completed a total of 15 rows. Wrap the back of the 15th row between rows 1 and 2 of the first woven circle (figure 3).

figure 2

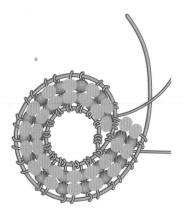

figure 3

4 Continue a two-sided flat weave with two bead rows for another 16 rows. The wraps of the back of each row are positioned between the rows of the previous woven circle. After finishing the back of the 31st row, wrap twice around the 20-gauge frame and trim off the remaining weaving wire (figure 4).

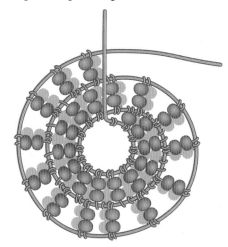

figure 4

5 Use chain nose pliers to make a 90° bend next to the anchor wraps. Trim the 20-gauge wire to ⅜ inch (1 cm), and use round-nose pliers to make a simple loop, turned toward the back of the pendant.

Weave the Petals

6 Coil 7 feet (2.1 m) of 26-gauge wire around the mandrel. Repeat to make a second coil. Cut a total of 20 coils, each ⅝ inch (1.6 cm) long.

7 Anchor wrap a 2½-foot (76.2 cm) piece of 26-gauge wire next to the last row of beads, with the tail away from the beads and the weaving wire close to the beads. Trim off the short tail.

8 Slide one of the ⅝-inch (1.6 cm) coils onto the weaving wire. Guide the wire up through the bottom, ⅜ inch (1.3 cm) away, working counterclockwise, and pull the wire taut, which will curve the coil into a petal shape. String another coil onto the weaving wire, and guide it up through the bottom, ⅜ inch (1.3 cm) away. Repeat six more times to add a total of seven petals around the outer ring (figure 5). After adding the seventh petal, anchor wrap twice, and trim off any remaining wire.

9 Use the remaining wire from the previous step to anchor wrap twice in the middle of the first petal. String one coil, guide the wire up through the bottom, ⅜ inch (1.3 cm) away, and pull the wire

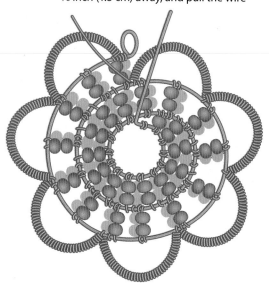

figure 5

taut. Add six more petals in the same manner. After adding the 14th (and last) petal, wrap the wire around the central 20-gauge wire. Leave the wire in place (figure 6).

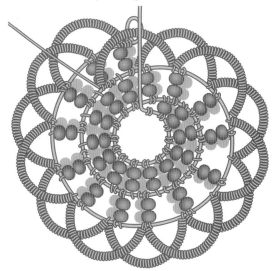

figure 6

10 String a coil onto the weaving wire, attach the next petal ¼ to ⅜ inches (0.6 to 1.3 cm) from the starting end, and wrap around the central 20-gauge wire. Repeat four more times, until the weaving wire is wrapped near to or around the innermost loop of 20-gauge wire (figure 7). Wrap twice and trim off any remaining wire.

figure 7

Add the Button

11 Slide the button onto the 2-inch (5.1 cm) piece of 20-gauge wire at the center of the flower. Bend the wire to position the button over the top of the center loop. Use chain-nose pliers to bend and feed the wire through to the back, directly across the loop (figure 8). Bend sharply against the center frame wire. Trim the wire to ¼ inch (6 mm), and tuck it against the back of the button. The button may move around slightly once it's anchored, which is perfectly fine.

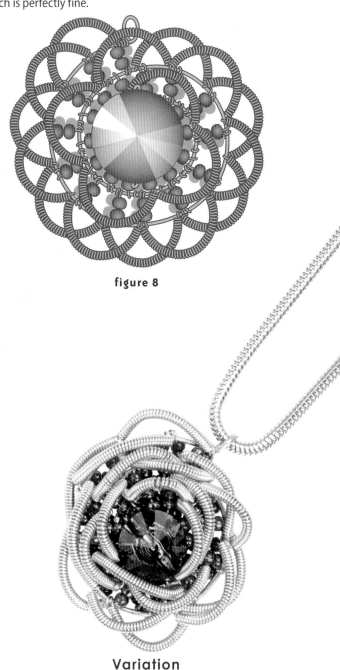

figure 8

Variation

Silver 20-gauge wire, 4 feet (1.2 m)

Silver 24-gauge wire, 22.5 feet (6.9m)

Aqua size 11° seed beads, 5 g

43 indicolite AB crystal bicones, 3 mm

28 light gray pearls, 3 mm

1 aquamarine crystal rivoli, 14 mm

9 silver 20-gauge jump rings, 3.5 mm inner diameter

Basic Tool Kit, page 11

0.04-inch (1 mm) mandrel

Micro torch

*Or add an additional 25 inches (63.5 cm) of silver 24-gauge wire if you want to make your own head pins.

FINISHED SIZE

2¾ inches (7 cm)

This pendant has many different components. They're labeled here to help you identify what you're making as you follow the instructions.

Arch
Dangle
Cluster
Leaf
Bail
Spring

PHOENIX RISING PENDANT

Blend together a unique group of elements, shapes, and techniques into an avant-garde pendant.

Arch

1 Cut two 3-inch (7.6 cm) lengths of 20-gauge wire. Mark both wires ¾ inch (1.9 cm) from one end.

2 Cut an 18-inch (45.7 cm) length of 24-gauge wire. Anchor wrap it twice around the mark on one piece of 20-gauge wire.

3 Begin a two-sided flat weave as follows. String one 11° seed bead, a bicone, and one seed bead onto the wire. Wrap the 24-gauge wire around the mark on the second piece of wire. String three seed beads, pull the wire back to the first wire, and wrap. Weave 12 more rows, for a total of 13, using the same pattern for all rows. After weaving the back of the 13th row, wrap the wire twice and trim off any excess.

4 Shape the woven portion into a horseshoe. Trim the wire ends ⅜ inch (1 cm) from the end wraps. Use round-nose pliers to make a simple loop, rolling backwards, toward the seed beads (figure 1).

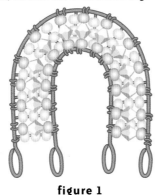

figure 1

Dangles and Clusters

If you prefer to make your own head pins instead of using commercial ones, cut twenty 1½-inch (3.8 cm) pieces of 24-gauge wire. Cut one 6-inch (15.2 cm) piece of 20-gauge wire. Cut three 1⅝-inch (1.6 cm) pieces of 20-gauge wire. Cut two 2-inch (5.1 cm) pieces of 20-gauge wire. Follow the instructions on page 25 to transform all the cut wires into head pins.

5 Make a dangle by stringing one bicone and one pearl onto a 1½-inch (3.8 cm) head pin. Use round-nose pliers to form a very small loop above the beads, wrap once, and trim off the excess wire. Repeat 19 more times to make a total of 20 dangles. Make four more dangles with a bicone and pearl on each, but make wraps above the bead. Set aside.

6 To make a cluster, string one bicone, one pearl, 10 of the dangles, and one pearl onto a 2-inch (5.1 cm) head pin. Make a wrapped loop above the top pearl, keeping the dangles tightly clustered as you wrap. Make a second cluster in the same manner (figure 2).

figure 2

Bezel the Rivoli

7 Cut 2 feet (61 cm) of 24-gauge wire. Make a bead stop at the end of the wire. String approximately 160 size 15° seed beads, or about 7½ inches (19 cm).

8 Mark ½ inch (1.3 cm) from the balled ends of three 1⅝-inch and one 6-inch, 20-gauge head pins. Bundle the head pins together, and wrap the 2-foot (61 cm) length of 24-gauge wire three times around the mark, wrapping toward the balled ends. Bend the head pins back to a 90° angle.

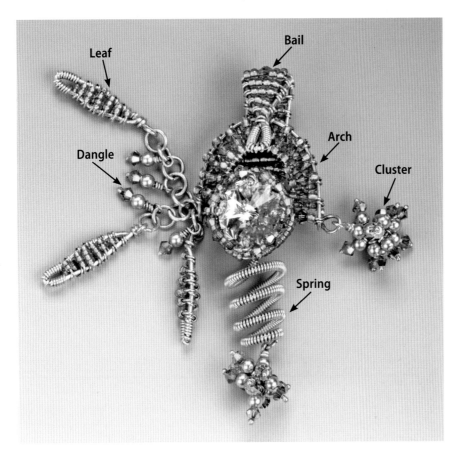

Leaf

Bail

Dangle

Arch

Cluster

Spring

9 Pull the 24-gauge wire over one of the head pins, and wrap completely around once, so the wire is beneath the head pins. String two size 15° seed beads, and make one wrap around the next head pin. Repeat between the other three head pins (figure 3). This is row 1.

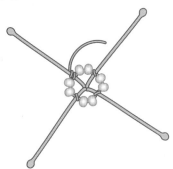

figure 3

10 Repeat step 9 four more times, adding two additional beads to each row. These rows form the base that holds the rivoli in place. They might need to be reshaped slightly to accommodate the point on the bottom of the rivoli. Set the rivoli on the base, and hold it in place. Use chain-nose pliers to bend the ends of the head pins over the top edge of the rivoli to form prongs.

11 Weave a sixth row, which should sit right on the bend in the prongs. It should contain 10 beads between each prong, just as in row 5.

12 The seventh row will sit over the top edge of the rivoli. Weave a size 15° seed bead, a bicone, a size 15° seed bead, a bicone, a size 15° seed bead, a bicone, and a size 15° seed bead between each prong. Wrap twice around the last prong. Push the prongs snug against

the rivoli. Unwrap the 24-gauge wire at the base of the bezel, and trim off any remaining wire (figure 4).

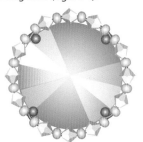

figure 4

Leaves

13 Wrap a 10-inch (25.4 cm) piece of 24-gauge wire 15 times around a 3-inch (7.6 cm) piece of 20-gauge wire. Cut off the short tail. String 30 size 15° seed beads onto the long wire, and make a bead stop at the end of the wire.

14 Fold the wire in half to form a U, and position the 24-gauge coil at the center of the 20-gauge wire. Keep the coil centered on the bend.

15 Begin a two-sided flat weave with a two-bead row. Wrap across the opposite side of the U, and weave a two-bead row behind the previous row. Continue to weave in the following pattern. Both sides of the weave use the same number of beads.

Row 2: three beads
Row 3: four beads
Row 4: three beads
Row 5: two beads
Row 6: one bead

16 After completing both sides of the sixth row, wrap twice around the 20-gauge wire, and trim off any remaining 24-gauge wire.

17 Cross one 20-gauge wire over the top of the other. To secure, wrap the top wire once around the bottom wire. Trim off the remaining end of the wrapped

wire. Trim the bottom wire to ¼ inch (6 mm). Use round-nose pliers to make a small round loop from the short tail (figure 5).

figure 5

18 Repeat steps 13 to 17 two more times to make a total of three leaves. Set them aside.

Bail

19 Anchor wrap a 2½-foot (76.2 cm) length of 24-gauge wire around a 6-inch (15.2 cm) length of 20-gauge wire. Wrap 25 times around the wire to form a ½-inch (2.5 cm) long coil. Trim off the short tail. Form the wire into a teardrop shape with the wires crossed at the top, and slide the coil to the center of the 20-gauge wire. Wrap the 24-gauge wire twice around both wires to secure them in place.

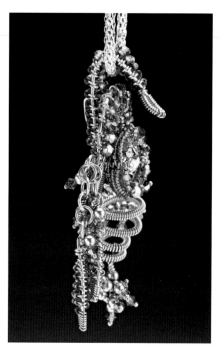

20 String 20 size 11° seed beads onto the 24-gauge wire, and make a bead stop at the end of the wire. Spread the two ends of the 20-gauge wire apart slightly, forming a V. Wrap the 24-gauge wire once around the 20-gauge wire nearest to you.

21 Position one seed bead in the V, and wrap around the opposite wire to begin a two-sided flat weave. Repeat across the back. Continue to weave three more rows, spreading the wires out as you go and adding one additional bead per row. After completing row 4, trim the bead stop off of the end of the weaving wire.

22 Rows 5 through 9 each have this pattern: On the front, string two size 15° seed beads, one bicone, and two 15° seed beads. On the back, string six 15° seed beads. Rows 10 through 15 consist of six 15° seed beads woven across both the front and back (figure 6). Wrap twice after completing row 15, and trim off the excess weaving wire.

figure 6

23 Trim the 20-gauge wires ⅜ inch (1 cm) from the last wraps. Use round-nose pliers to make a simple loop on each end, rolling the loops toward the back of the bail.

Assemble

24 Position the rivoli with the long tail pointing down. Grasp the head pin at the top of the rivoli, and bend it back 90° so that it points directly backward from the center of the bezel. Open the loops on the arch, and slide it around the head pins extending horizontally from the rivoli. Position the arch behind the rivoli, and make sure all of the loops are closed (figure 7).

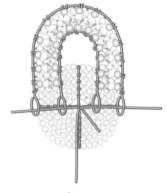

figure 7

25 Open the loops of the bail, and attach it to the same horizontal wires as the arch. Position the hanger behind the arch, with the crystals on the back, and make sure both of the loops are closed. When you shape the hanger, the crystals will end up on the front of the pendant.

26 From the beadwork, measure ⅝ inch (1.6 cm) along the wire coming out of the center of the back, and make a 90° bend at the mark. Press the wire into the back of the hanger, pushing it between the 10th and 11th rows. It may be necessary to adjust the angle of the bend if needed, to keep the wire in position at the back of the pendant.

27 Trim the horizontal head pin wires to ⅜ inch (1 cm) past the loops of the arch. Use round-nose pliers to shape each end into a simple loop.

28 Gently bend the bail toward the front, lining up the second crystal in the center at the top of the hanger. Grasp the loop of the hanger using round-nose pliers, and curve the hook forward.

Back

29 Now you'll make the spring. Coil 3 feet (91.4 cm) of 24-gauge wire around the mandrel, creating a coil about 4½ inches (11.4 cm) long. Trim off the wire ends. Trim the coil to 4 inches (10.2 cm), and slide it on the remaining long head pin on the pendant.

30 Slide a mandrel or round object about ¼ inch (6 mm) in diameter behind the pendant. Push the coil up against the rivoli, and wrap the coil-clad head-pin around the mandrel three or four times. Remove the mandrel and refine the shape by hand until you're satisfied with it. Trim the 20-gauge wire extending from the coil to ⅜ inch (1 cm), and use round-nose pliers to form a simple loop. Use the round-nose pliers to center the loop by turning in the same direction (figure 8). Use chain-nose pliers to open the loop, and then attach one of the clusters. Close the loop.

Variations

figure 8

31 Use chain-nose pliers to open the loop on the right hand side of the arch, attach one of the clusters, and close the loop.

32 Following along with figure 9, attach the leaf shapes in the loop on the left side of the arch as follows.

• Attach one jump ring to the top loop of a leaf shape, insert a dangle into the ring, and attach the ring to the loop (this element is labeled A).

• Attach an empty jump ring to a second jump ring with a dangle, and then add a third jump ring and attach the dangle to the left of the previous leaf dangle (this element is labeled B).

• Link a total of five rings, catching a dangle into both the second and fourth rings, and then use a sixth ring to attach all three dangles together, and to the loop on the arch (this element is labeled C).

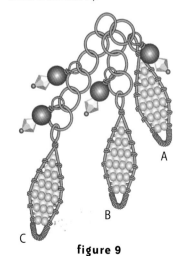

A

B

C

figure 9

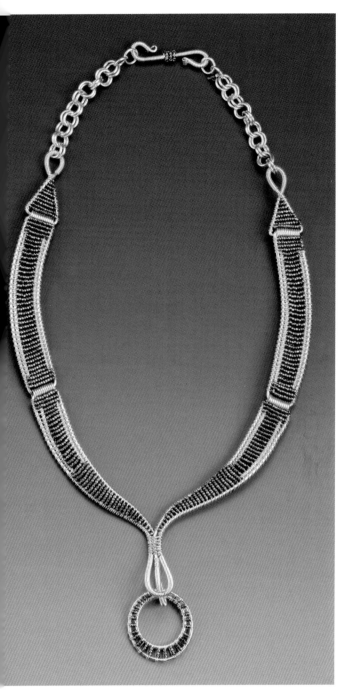

Necklaces

You'll feel like a queen wearing a necklace named after Nefertiti or Cleopatra.

SUPPLIES

Silver 16-gauge wire, 13½ inches (34.3 cm)

Silver 22-gauge wire, 8 feet (2.4 m)

Silver 24-gauge wire, 2 feet (61 cm)

Purple iris size 11° round seed beads, 2 g

1 dark purple pearl, 5 mm

54 silver jump rings, 18 gauge, 5 mm inner diameter

Basic Tool Kit, page 11

0.05-inch (1.3 mm) mandrel

FINISHED SIZE

22 inches (55.9 cm) long

INTERCHANGEABLE NECKLACE

Create a clean, modern neck wire with great structure, an elegant line, and a hint of color. This is the perfect way to turn any pendant or focal component into a finished necklace that's as versatile as it is beautiful.

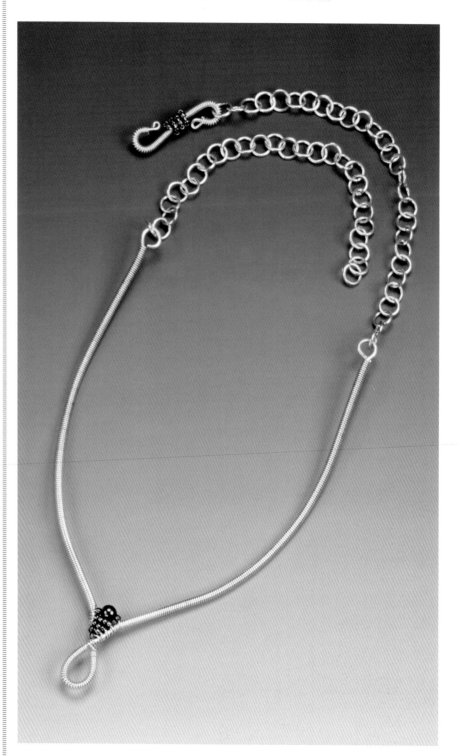

1 Leaving a ½-inch (1.3 cm) tail, wrap the 24-gauge wire around a 13½-inch (34.3 cm) piece of 16-gauge wire 48 times, or until the coil is roughly 1¼ inches (3.2 cm) long, and leave the end attached. Slide the coil to the middle of the 16-gauge wire, and shape it into a U. As shown in figure 1, cross the 16-gauge wire over itself, turning the U into a teardrop-shaped loop. Wrap the 24-gauge wire three times around the point where the 16-gauge wire crosses itself.

figure 1

90

2 Make a bead stop at the end of the wire. String 20 seed beads onto the 24-gauge wire. Make one complete wrap around the 16-gauge wire nearest to you.

3 Begin a two-sided flat weave with a single bead row that fits between the wires at the point above the loop. Add one bead to each of the next three rows until you've woven both sides of four rows. After finishing the back of the fourth row, wrap three times around the 16-gauge wire. Trim off the bead stop, and string on a seed bead, the pearl, and one more seed bead. Weave these three beads across the front half of the fifth row. Wrap twice around the 16-gauge wire, and trim off any remaining weaving wire (figure 2).

4 Coil 8 feet (2.5 m) of 22-gauge wire around the mandrel. Remove the coil from the mandrel, cut it in half, and trim the ends neatly. Slide a coil onto each half of the 16-gauge wire. Trim both of the wires ⅝ inch (1.6 cm) past the end of the coil. Use round-nose pliers to form the ends of the 16-gauge wire into simple round loops. Shape the wire to curve gently away from the center, making it straighter near the top (figure 3).

5 Referring to page 23, make two sections of 1-in-1 jump-ring chain, each 27 rings long. Attach one chain to each end of the neck wire.

6 Follow the instructions on page 23 to make a hook clasp, stringing on 19 seed beads to form the beaded coil at the center of the clasp. Attach the clasp to the end the chain.

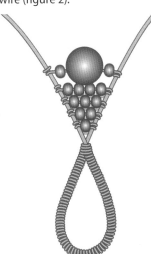

figure 2

Variation

figure 3

SUPPLIES

Silver 16-gauge wire, 8 feet (2.4 m)

Silver 20-gauge wire, 2 feet (61 cm)

Silver 26-gauge wire, 38 feet (11.6 m)

Gold-filled 24-gauge wire, 1 foot (30.5 cm)

Topaz AB size 15° round seed beads, 10 g

44 silver jump rings, 18 gauge, 5 mm inner diameter

Basic Tool Kit, page 11

Mandrels:

  ⅔ inch (9 mm)

  0.05 inch (1.3 mm)

  1 inch (2.5 cm)

  ¾-inch (1.9 cm)

Micro torch

FINISHED SIZE

23 inches (58.4 cm) long

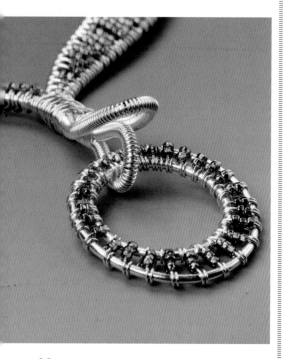

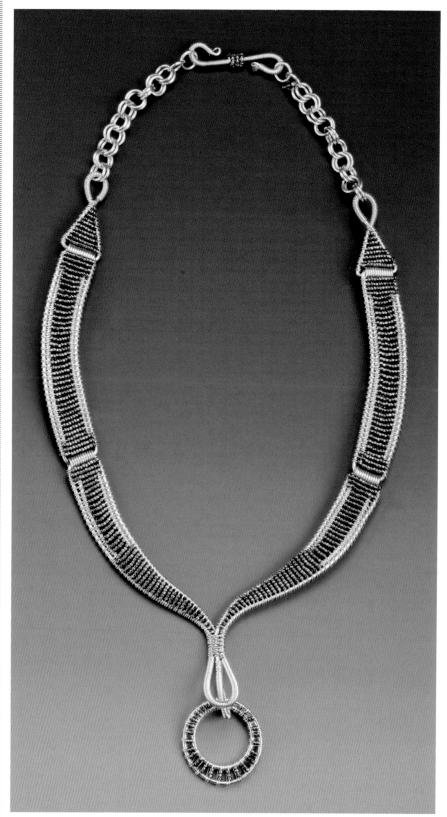

NEFERTITI NECKLACE

Multiple hinges allow this necklace to rest comfortably and gracefully around the neck. An Egyptian-inspired circle pendant dangles from the tapered point.

Prepare the Coils

1 Coil 2 feet (61 cm) of 20-gauge wire around the ⅔-inch (9 mm) mandrel. Trim the finished coil into four ⅜-inch (1 cm) sections. Leaving a 5-inch (12.7 cm) tail, wrap 4 feet (1.2 m) of 26-gauge wire around the 0.05-inch (1.3 mm) mandrel. Leave the tail attached to the beginning of the coil, and trim two 1-inch (2.5 cm) coils off the end of the coil. The beginning coil with the attached tail should measure approximately 1 inch (2.5 cm); if it's longer, trim any extra length off the end with no tail.

Circle Pendant

2 To make the small ring, form 2⅜ inches (6 cm) of 16-gauge wire around the mandrel with a ¾-inch (1.9 cm) diameter. Form 3⅛ inches (8 cm) of the same wire around the mandrel with a 1-inch (2.5 cm) diameter. Solder the two rings (page 26).

3 Cut 30 inches (76.2 cm) of 26-gauge wire. Make a bead stop at one end of the wire, and string on 44 seed beads. Anchor wrap around the small soldered ring. Place the small ring inside of the large ring, hold one seed bead between the two rings, and make one full wrap around the large ring. Weave back across to the small ring, leaving an exposed wire between the two rings, and begin a single-sided flat weave, with each bead row ¹⁄₁₆ inch (1.6 mm) or slightly farther from the adjacent rows. Rows 1 to 9 have one seed bead. For rows 10 to 14, use two seed beads. Step up to three seed beads across rows 15 to 24. Taper back down to two seed beads for rows 25 to 29. After completing the back of row 29, wrap twice around the outer circle and trim off any remaining wire (figure 1).

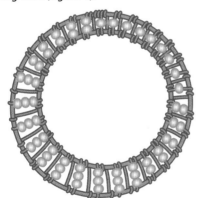

figure 1

4 Cut two pieces of 16-gauge wire, each 10½ inches (26.7 cm) long. Mark the exact center of each wire, and then mark ⅞ inch (2.2 cm) from the center on both sides. Slide the coil with the tail attached to the center of the 16-gauge wire. Keeping the coil centered, fold the 16-gauge wire into a U shape. Use chain-nose pliers to bend the wire slightly, next to the coil, on each side. Insert the circle pendant into the U. Use the tail wire to wrap nine times around both halves of the 16-gauge wire. Trim off any excess wire (figure 2).

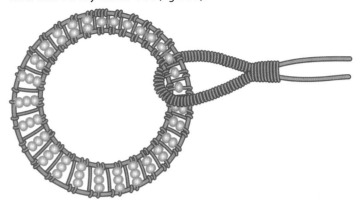

figure 2

5 Center a 1-inch (2.5 cm) coil from step 1 on the remaining 10½-inch (26.7 cm) piece of 16-gauge wire. As in the previous step, fold the 16-gauge wire into a U. Anchor wrap a 1-foot (30.5 cm) piece of 24-gauge gold-filled wire onto the 16-gauge wire and slide it next to the coil at the center. Pull the sides of the 16-gauge wire inward, and position the U around the loop holding the pendant. Place the U in front of the woven circle. Alternate the wires from the loop and the U, and form a neat bundle. Begin a tubular weave with the bare wire. Make one full wrap around each of the four wires. Wrap a total of six rows onto each of the wires. Wrap twice after finishing the last row (figure 3). Trim off the wire tails.

figure 3

Shape and Weave the Necklace

6 Cut two pieces of 26-gauge wire, each 5½ feet (1.7 m) long. Make a bead stop on one end and string 8½ inches (21.6 cm) of seed beads.

7 Split the four pieces of 16-gauge wire into pairs above the woven section. Each pair uses a wire from each of the loops in front. Shape the wires out from the center, and form a curve with a gap between the wires. Position the tail of the wire with the strung beads next to the center, and anchor wrap it on the upper 16-gauge wire.

8 Position one seed bead in the V formed by the two wires, and begin a two-sided flat weave, as follows. The first four rows have one seed bead. Add an additional bead to the count in these rows: row 5, row 8, row 11, row 14, row 17, row 20, and at row 23, the widest row, increase to eight beads.

9 Cut four 2½-inch (6.4 cm) pieces of 16-gauge wire. Insert one piece next to the woven portion, and position it next to the inside of the frame wire. Wrap from the frame wire around the newly added wire. Position five beads next to the second frame wire, position a second 2½-inch (6.4 cm) piece to the inside of the opposite frame wire, and wrap once around the new wire. Make one complete wrap around the outer wire, and one complete wrap around the inner wire, then string five more beads. Wrap around the opposite inner wire, and wrap around the adjacent outer wire.

10 Repeat nine more times, until 10 rows, front and back, are completed. As you do so, continue to shape the frame wires into a curve. On the inside curve, make a mark 2⅛ inches (5.4 cm) from the first woven row. Make a mark on the outside curve perpendicular to the mark on the inside curve. Trim both of the inner wires ⅛ inch (3 mm) short of the marks, and leave the outer wires intact. At each mark, use chain-nose pliers to make a 90° bend toward

the center. Trim the wires ³⁄₁₆ inch (5 mm) from the bend (figure 4).

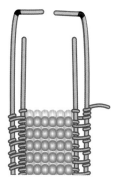

figure 4

11 Slide a ⅜-inch (1 cm) coil from step 1 onto both of the short ends. Push the ends inward. Weave six more rows between the doubled frame wires. Weave three more rows, each consisting of nine beads front and back, from outside wire to outside wire. Complete the last row, wrap twice, and trim off any remaining wire.

12 Weave the opposite side of the front of the necklace.

13 Cut two pieces of 16-gauge wire, each 8 inches (20.3 cm) long. Mark the wires 3½ inches (8.9 cm) from one end, and use chain-nose pliers to make a 90° bend at each mark. Insert the long end of the wire through one of the coils attached in step 11. Use chain-nose pliers to grasp the 16-gauge wire where it comes out of the coil, and make a 90° bend as close as possible to the coil.

14 Make a bead stop on a 7½-inch (19 cm) piece of 26-gauge wire, and string 11 inches (27.9 cm) of seed beads. Anchor wrap the wire around the inner 16-gauge wire next to one of the coils added in step 11. Begin a two-sided flat weave with a 10-bead row. Weave two additional rows, each nine beads in length, front and back.

15 Cut four pieces of 16-gauge wire, each 3 inches (7.6 cm) long. Attach the piece in the same manner as in step 9. Weave six beads across, and insert the second piece of wire. Use the flat weave described in step 9 to weave the front and back of 25 rows. Shape the wires as you weave to create a curved section.

16 Measure and mark the inside wire 2⅝ inches (6.7 cm) from the beginning of the six-bead rows. Place a ruler across the section in a perpendicular position, and mark the outside wire. Trim both of the inside wires ⅛ inch (3 mm) short of the marks on the outside wires. Use chain-nose pliers to bend the outside wires 90° at the mark, toward the center. Trim each wire ³⁄₁₆ inch (5 mm) from the corner. Slide a ⅜-inch (1 cm) coil onto the ³⁄₁₆-inch (5 mm) ends, and push the sides inward to lock the coil in place.

17 Weave six more six-bead rows, front and back, between the two wires. Weave three additional rows of nine beads each, weaving over the ends of the inner 16-gauge wires. After the final row, make two wraps and trim off any remaining weaving wire (figure 5).

figure 5

18 Repeat steps 13 to 17 to weave the other side of the necklace.

End Connectors

19 Cut two pieces of 16-gauge wire, each 4 inches (10.2 cm) long. Mark the center, and then ³⁄₈ inch (1 cm) from the center mark on both sides. Coil a 2½-inch (6.4 cm) piece of 26-gauge wire 50 times around one of the 16-gauge wires. Cut off the short tail from the beginning and leave the long length attached.

20 Position the coil between the marks on either side of the center, and fold the 16-gauge wire into a U. Cross the 16-gauge wire over itself, and then wrap the 26-gauge wire around both wires three times where the wires cross. Make a mark ⁵⁄₈ inch (1.6 cm) from the last wrap of weaving wire on both sides. Use chain-nose pliers to bend both wires 90° inward at the marks. Trim each wire ³⁄₁₆ inch (5 mm) from the bend. Insert the ends into the ³⁄₈-inch (1 cm) coil at the back of the previous section.

21 Make one more full wrap around the left 16-gauge wire. String 26 seed beads onto the wire, and make a bead stop at the end of the wire. Begin a two-sided flat weave with a single-bead row. Add one bead for each row through row 5, which will be five beads wide. Weave seven beads across row 6. Add two beads for a total of nine across row 7, and then add one bead per row for rows 8 and 9, which will be 11 beads across. After weaving both sides of row 9, wrap twice and trim off the remaining weaving wire (figure 6).

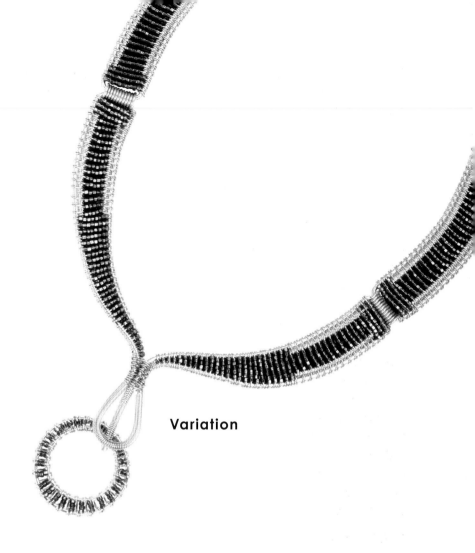

Variation

figure 6

22 Repeat steps 19 to 21 to complete the other side of the necklace.

Clasp and Chain

23 Follow the instructions starting on page 23 to make a wire hook clasp.

24 Open half of the jump rings and close the other half. Attach two rings through each of the end connectors. From these two rings, add nine more pairs of rings to create a 2-in-2 jump-ring chain (page 23) that's 10 pairs of rings long. Attach two single rings to the end of each chain. On one side, attach the clasp to the single jump ring on the end of the chain.

MOROCCAN JEWELS NECKLACE

Triangles encrusted with beads encircle the neck, glinting with every movement like exotic jewels found in the markets of Marrakesh.

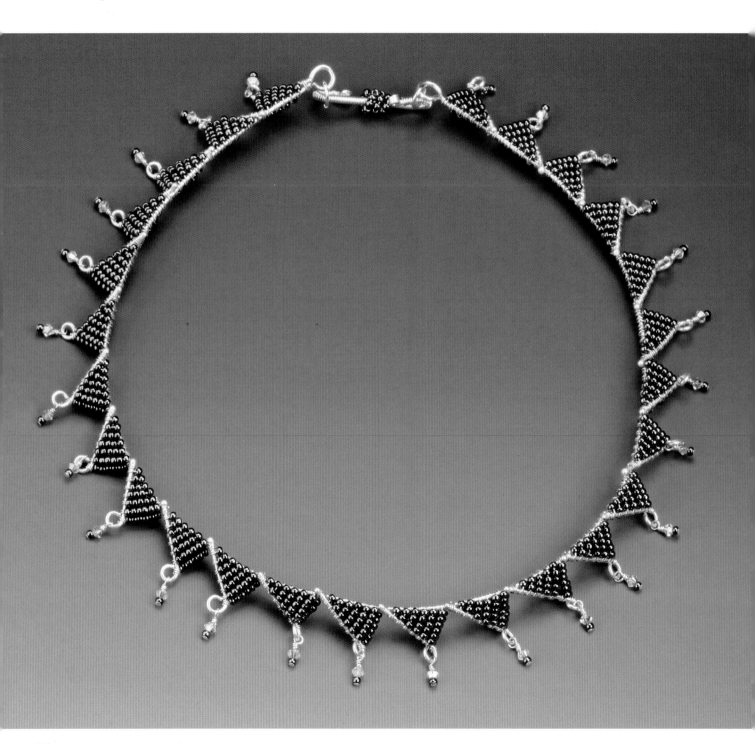

Make Head Pins

1 Refer to the instructions on page 25 to make 26 silver head pins out of the 18-gauge wire, each 1½ inches (3.8 cm) long. **Note:** This quantity is for a 17½-inch (44.5 cm) necklace. For each additional ½ inch (13 mm) of length desired, make one additional 18-gauge head pin and purchase one additional 24-gauge head pin. Be aware that the clasp adds 1¼ inches (3.2 cm) to the overall length.

Weave the Necklace

2 As shown in figure 1, hold the ball end of a head pin over the 16-gauge wire in your non-dominant hand, angled to create a wedge shape. Using the 26-gauge wire, anchor wrap the head pin twice to the neck wire, then wrap twice around just the head pin (figure 1).

figure 1

3 Begin a two-sided flat weave, starting with a single-bead row, front and back. Add one bead to each consecutive row, until six rows are complete, front and back, with the widest row containing six beads. After the sixth row is complete, anchor wrap the weaving wire twice, and trim off any remaining wire (figure 2).

figure 2

4 Trim the remaining 18-gauge head pin wire ⅜ inch (1 cm) from the sixth row. Use round nose pliers to form a round loop as shown in figure 3. You've now finished a beaded triangle.

figure 3

SUPPLIES

Silver 16-gauge wire, 2 feet (61 cm)

Silver 18-gauge wire, 39 inches (1 m)*

Silver 26-gauge wire, 28 feet (8.5 m)

Dark green metallic size 11° seed beads, 10 g

26 peridot AB crystal bicones, 3 mm

2 silver jump rings, 18 gauge, 6 mm inner diameter

26 silver head pins, 24 gauge, 1½ inches (3.8 cm)

***Necklaces larger than 17½ inches (44.5 cm) may require up to 4 feet (1.2 m) of 18-gauge wire. Also, see the note at the end of step 1.**

Basic Tool Kit, page 11

Micro torch

FINISHED SIZE

17½ inches (44.5 cm)

5 One angle of the beaded triangle consists of where the balled end of the head pin intersects with the 16-gauge wire. That angle points toward one end of the 16-gauge wire. Mark that end of the 16-gauge wire ⅝ inch (1.6 cm) from the tip, and form that length of wire into a large round loop. Slide the triangle completed in step 4 as close as possible to the loop (figure 4).

6 Repeat steps 2 through 4 until the desired length is achieved. As you finish each triangle, position it snugly against the previous triangle, and then make the next one.

7 Shape the beadwork into a large circle to fit around the neck. Cut the 16-gauge wire ⅝ inch (1.6 cm) from the sixth row of the last beaded triangle. Use round-nose pliers to form a large round loop.

8 Make as many dangle elements as you have triangles. Each dangle consists of one size 11° seed bead and one bicone strung on a 24-gauge head pin, with a wire-wrapped loop above the beads. Use chain-nose pliers to open the loop on each triangle, insert one dangle, and then close the loop again.

9 Follow the instructions on page 23 to make a wire hook clasp. Attach the clasp with a single jump ring to the large loops on each end of the neck wire.

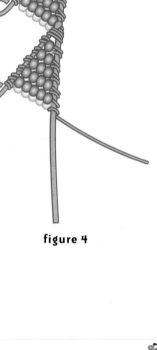

figure 4

Variation

SUPPLIES

Silver 20-gauge wire, 9 feet (2.8 m)

Silver 26-gauge wire, 27 feet (8.2 m)

Size 15° round seed beads:

> **Gold, 6 g**

> **Silver, 6 g**

7 lampworked beads, 12 mm with ⅛-inch (3 mm) bead hole

65 jump rings, 18 gauge, 5 mm inner diameter

Basic Tool Kit, page 11

FINISHED SIZE

18 inches (45.7 cm)

1 Cut 24 pieces of 26-gauge wire, each 12 inches (30.5 cm) long. Make a bead stop on the end of each piece. String the following pattern onto each of the weaving wires:

- one gold, one silver
- two gold, two silver
- three gold, three silver
- four gold, four silver
- five gold, five silver
- six gold, six silver
- five gold, five silver
- four gold, four silver
- three gold, three silver
- two gold, two silver
- one gold, one silver

2 Cut four pieces of 20-gauge wire, each 14 inches (35.6 cm) long, and 24 more pieces, each 2 inches (5.1 cm) long. Mark one of the long wires 2½ inches (6.4 cm) from the end. Mark one short piece of wire ½ inch (1.3 cm) from the end.

3 Position one long and one short piece next to each other, with the marks aligned. Anchor wrap one of the 26-gauge wires prepared in step 1 around both 20-gauge wires. Position the wraps on the marks.

4 Use chain-nose pliers to bend the short, or outer wire, creating a 30° angle (figure 1).

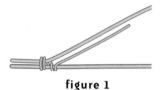

figure 1

5 Wrap the weaving wire once around the longer piece of 20-gauge wire, which is the inner wire.

6 Begin a two-sided flat weave by positioning the first seed bead in the point between the two wires. Make one complete wrap around the outer wire. Continue the two-sided flat weave until you've woven six beads across both sides. *Note:* Because of the way the beads were strung, each side of the weave is a different color.

7 Position your chain-nose pliers next to the sixth row, and bend the short outer wire back down toward the inner wire. This will form a triangle.

8 From this point, the two-sided flat weave continues in reverse. The next row has five beads, then four beads, and so on, making each row one bead shorter until you reach the other point of the triangle. After weaving the last single bead in position, make two anchor wraps with the 26-gauge wire. Trim off the weaving wires on both sides of the triangle.

9 Measure ¹⁄₁₆ inch (1.6 mm) past the anchor wraps, and cut off the remaining outer (short) piece of 20-gauge wire (figure 2). Repeat on the other end of the outer wire. Set aside the first prepared wire.

figure 2

10 Repeat steps 3 through 9 three more times to prepare a total of four triangles on four separate 14-inch (35.6 cm) pieces of 20-gauge wire.

11 Slide a glass bead onto one of the four wires, positioning the bead next to the triangle. Repeat steps 3 through 9 to create a second triangle on the 14-inch (35.6 cm) wire. Push the lampworked bead close to the first triangle (figure 3).

figure 3

12 Take the second of the four wires prepared in step 10, and slide it through the lampworked bead, then position the second triangle next to the first one. Repeat steps 3 through 9 to weave a second triangle on the second wire. Half of the first diamond is now complete (figure 4).

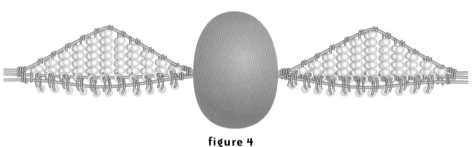

figure 4

13 Slide the third of the four wires prepared in step 10 through the lampworked bead. Position the third triangle next to the second one, being sure to arrange the colors as desired. Repeat steps 3 through 10 to weave a third triangle on the third wire.

14 Take the last of the four wires prepared in step 11 and slide it through the lampworked bead. Push the lampworked bead up against the other three triangles, completing the first diamond (figure 5). Repeat steps 3 through 10 to weave a fourth triangle onto the fourth wire.

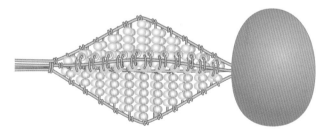

figure 5

15 Push the lampworked bead up against the first triangle. Push the second set of triangles close to the first ones. Slide another lampworked bead onto all four of the wires with two diamonds woven in place.

Variations

16 Continue to weave triangles and add lampworked beads until six diamonds are complete (figure 6).

figure 6

17 On each end, there will be four wires sticking out of a diamond. Both ends are finished in the same way, as follows. Choose one of the four wires, and wrap it twice around the other three wires (figure 7). Flush cut the tail off of the wrapped wire, and leave the other three wires intact.

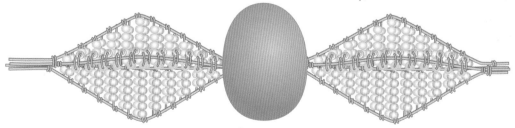

figure 7

18 Slide one lampworked bead onto the three wires, and snug it up against the wraps. Choose one of the three wires and wrap it around the other two. Flush cut the tail off of the wrapped wire. Choose one of the two remaining wires, and flush cut the tail right next to the wraps (figure 8). Leave one wire intact.

figure 8

19 Make sure all the diamonds and lampworked beads are snug against each other. Form a wrapped loop with the last remaining wire. After wrapping both ends, shape the beads and triangles into a curve.

20 A basic 2-in-1 jump-ring chain (page 23) provides the additional length between the end loop and wire hook clasp. Make equally long sections of it on both sides of the necklace until you've achieved the desired length, making sure each chain ends with a single ring. Make a wire hook clasp (page 23), using either color of seed beads for the wrapped beads in the middle of the clasp, and attach it to the loose end of either one of the chains.

Silver 16-gauge wire, 2½ inches
(6.4 cm)

Silver 20-gauge wire, 3 feet (91.4 cm)

Silver 22-gauge wire, 6 feet (1.8 m)

Silver 26-gauge wire, 17 feet (5.2 m)

1 rose AB crystal rivoli, 18 mm

Burgundy metallic size 15° seed beads,
15 g

38 metallic blue crystal bicones, 3 mm

19 fuchsia crystal bicones, 5 mm

21 silver head pins, 24 gauge,
1½ inches (3.8 cm)

6 silver jump rings, 20 gauge, 4 mm
inner diameter

42 silver jump rings, 20 gauge, 7 mm
inner diameter

Basic Tool Kit, page 11

FINISHED SIZE

21½ inches (54.6 cm) long
Focal element, 2½ x 2¾ inches
(6.4 x 7 cm)

WIRE-GO-ROUND NECKLACE

**Weave a web of wire circles into a whimsical, lively freeform necklace.
Finish with an elegant link chain highlighted with beads.**

Bezel the Rivoli

1 Referring to the instructions starting on page 20, create a bezel for the 18-mm rivoli, using 3 feet (91.4 cm) of both 20- and 26-gauge wire. Weave one row on the front with seed beads, then weave two bare wire rows that sit along the side, and then weave one row on the back to hold the rivoli in place, for a total of four rows. Trim only the wire attached to the front of the bezel to ⅜ inch (1 cm), and use it to create a loop. (This is the loop from which you'll hang three dangles in a later step.)

Weave the Circles

2 Working with the 20-gauge wire still attached to the back of the bezel, use round-nose pliers to make a loop about ½ inch (1.3 cm) from the bezel. Bring the tail over the top of the loop (figure 1). Make a bead stop on a 1-foot (25.4 cm) piece of 26-gauge wire, and string 12 size 15° seed beads. Anchor wrap the 26-gauge wire around the 20-gauge wire inside of the loop, where the wires overlap, with the tail coming up through the loop.

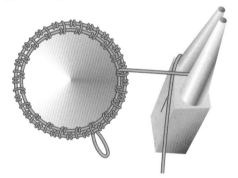

figure 1

3 Begin a single-sided flat weave by weaving one bead in the space between the two wires (figure 2). Weave the bare wire across the back, and return to the smaller loop. Shape the 20-gauge wire into a circle and continue to weave

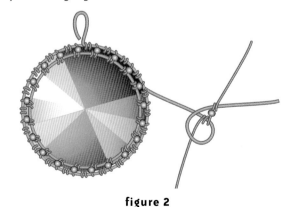

figure 2

single-bead rows. Weave around in a full circle, about 11 or 12 rows, back to the starting point (figure 3).

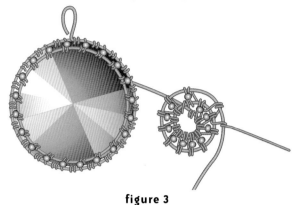

figure 3

4 To add a second ring to the outside, this one without beads, shape the 20-gauge wire around the outside row. Weave between the second and third rings with bare wire and no beads, back to the starting point where the innermost loop starts. Wrap the 26-gauge weaving wire twice around the 20-gauge wire, and trim off any remaining wire (figure 4). You've completed the first circle.

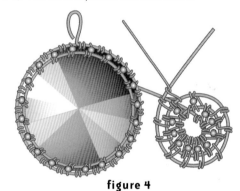

figure 4

5 To begin another circle, use round-nose pliers to form the 20-gauge wire into a loop about ⅜ inch (1 cm) from the previous circle, crossing the tail wire over the top of the loop (figure 5). Begin to weave as described in step 2, starting with the same length of 26-gauge wire, then feel free to make the design your own, creating another 11 circles that

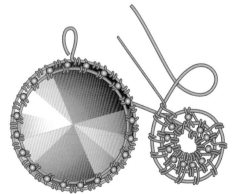

figure 5

vary in size and number of rows. Some should consist of two loops and others of three loops, and the rows can be one or two beads wide. Be fearless, and customize the design as you work. At the start of each circle, shape the 20-gauge wire so that, as a group, the first six or seven circles form into a curve under the rivoli (figure 6).

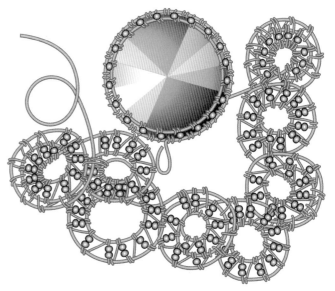

figure 6

6 Arrange the woven pieces into a pleasing shape, and position the loop on the rivoli toward the bottom. At the point where the seventh circle touches the rivoli bezel, give the shape some structure by using a 3-inch (7.6 cm) piece of 26-gauge wire to attach the outside wire of the circle to a spot on the back of the bezel (figure 7). To strengthen the other portions of the design, anchor circles to previous circles, or to other spots where two circles intersect or sit close together.

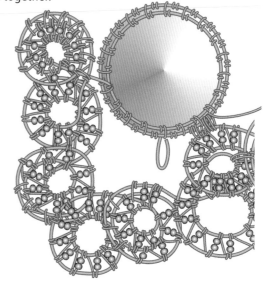

figure 7

Variation

Add Fringe

7 Create seven long dangle elements; for each, string one size 15° seed bead, one 3-mm bicone, and one 5-mm bicone on a head pin and make a wire-wrapped loop at the top. Make 14 short dangle elements; each consists of one size 15° seed bead and one 3-mm bicone on a head pin with a wire-wrapped loop above the beads. Open one jump ring, and string one short, one long, and one short dangle into the ring, and close the jump ring. Open the loop on the bezel, insert the single ring holding the dangle elements, and close the loop.

8 Open five jump rings, and string one long and two short dangles into each. Assemble these embellished rings into a section of chain. Use a sixth open jump ring to attach the top ring of the embellished chain to the circle at the very bottom of the necklace. Before you close this jump ring, catch one long and two short dangles in it.

Create a Clasp

9 Follow the instructions on page 23 to make a wire hook clasp. In the center of the clasp, use the same color beads as you used to make the circles.

Make the Chain

10 Use 22-gauge wire to make 12 links. Each link consists of a wire-wrapped loop, a 3-mm bicone, a 5-mm bicone, a 3-mm bicone, and a second wire wrapped loop. You will make the chain in two halves, as follows. Attach two linked jump rings to each of the circles that sit highest up on the left and right sides. Add one more jump ring, plus one of the beaded links. Join each link to the next using three jump rings, until you've used six links.

If the finished pendant hangs at a slight angle, correct the problem by making the shorter half of the chain one link longer than the other. End one half with three rings, and attach the clasp to the other half of the chain.

Back

SUPPLIES

Silver 16-gauge wire, 2 feet (61 cm)

Silver 18-gauge wire, 5½ feet (1.7 m)

Silver 20-gauge wire, 1 foot (30.5 cm)

Silver 26-gauge wire, 24 feet (7.3 m)

Bronze metallic size 11° seed beads, 10 g

602 bronze keishi pearls, 6–7 mm

292 Bali flower spacers, 5 mm

18 silver head pins, 24 gauge, 1½ inches (3.8 cm)

1 elongated lampworked bead, 3 inches (7.6 cm)

1 Bali silver bead cap, 7 mm

1 round focal bead, 24 mm

3 jump rings, 18 gauge, 7 mm inner diameter

Basic Tool kit, page 11

Micro torch

FINISHED SIZE

17½ inches (44.5 cm)

DREAMSCAPE NECKLACE

Envision a merger of shapely glass beads, a textured wheel, and keishi pearl-studded dimensional straps.

Solder the Rings

1 Make two circles from two 2-inch (5.1 cm) pieces of 16-gauge wire, and one circle from a 5-inch (12.7-cm) piece of wire. Refer to the instructions on page 26 to solder all three rings closed.

Build the Wheel

2 Anchor wrap a 3½-foot (1 m) length of 26-gauge wire around one of the small rings, leaving a ½-inch (1.3 cm) tail attached. String on three size 11° seed beads, and make one complete wrap around the second small circle (figure 1).

figure 1

3 String on one size 11° seed bead, one keishi pearl, one Bali flower spacer, two keishi pearls, one Bali flower spacer, one keishi pearl, and one size 11° seed bead. Make one complete wrap around the large ring (figure 2). Repeat the same stringing

figure 2

pattern, and make one complete wrap around the first small ring (figure 3).

figure 3

4 String three size 11° seed beads, and make one complete wrap around the second small ring.

5 Repeat steps 3 and 4 for a total of 13 rows, front and back. Try to keep the rows as straight as possible while weaving. After the last row is complete, wrap twice around the small circle, and trim off any remaining wire (figure 4).

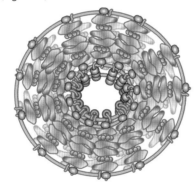

figure 4

Preparing the Long Bead

6 Prepare seven dangles. Each dangle consists of one size 11° seed bead and one keishi pearl strung on a 1½-inch (3.8 cm) head pin, with a wire-wrapped loop above the beads.

7 Cut a piece of 20-gauge wire three times longer than the elongated lampworked bead. Use chain-nose pliers to make a U-shaped bend in the middle of the wire. String the dangles

prepared in step 6 into the U. Slide both ends of the wire up through the lampworked bead. Above the bead, wrap one piece of the 20-gauge wire around the other piece twice. Trim off the end of the wrapped wire. Slide a Bali bead cap onto the remaining wire to cover the wrap, and make a wire-wrapped loop above the bead cap.

8 Next, you'll make double-ended head pins to use as core wires for the straps. Cut four pieces of 18-gauge wire 8¼ inches (21-cm) long, and draw both ends into a ball with a torch. Cut four 8-inch (20.3-cm) pieces of wire, and ball all the ends.

Weave the Double-Cone Strap

9 Make a bead stop on 3 feet (90.5 cm) of 26-gauge wire, and string on 132 size 11° seed beads. Position two longer wires cut in step 8 next to one another, and then two shorter wires. Anchor wrap the 26-gauge wire around any one of the core wires, and begin to weave a tube (pages 19-20) as follows. First, weave a total of three two-bead rows. Add one more seed bead, and weave five rows of three seed beads. Weave rows 9 through 11 with four seed beads (figure 5).

figure 5

Variation

10 Continuing the tubular weave, start a new pattern at row 12, as follows: one size 11° seed bead, one keishi pearl, one Bali spacer, one keishi pearl, and one size 11° seed bead. Continue this pattern all the way to row 40.

11 At row 41, begin to narrow the tube back into a cone shape by weaving four size 11° seed beads. For rows 42 and 43, weave three seed beads. Weave two seed beads for rows 44 through 48. The last eight rows of weaving require ¾ inch (1.9 cm) of space. Because keishi pearls vary in size, you may have to add or subtract one or two rows to fill the core wires completely. After you complete the last row, wrap the weaving wire twice around the nearest core wire, and trim off any remaining wire.

Weave the Single-Cone Strap

12 Repeat step 9, and then continue the tubular weave pattern through row 39. For row 40, string one size 11° seed bead, one keishi pearl, one Bali flower spacer, one keishi pearl, and one size 11° seed bead. On row 43, string one size 11° seed bead, three keishi pearls, and one size 11° seed bead. Finish with rows 44 through 48, which consist of one size 11° seed bead, two keishi pearls, one Bali flower spacer, two keishi pearls, and one size 11° seed bead. After you complete the last row, wrap the weaving wire twice around the nearest core wire and trim off any remaining wire (figure 6).

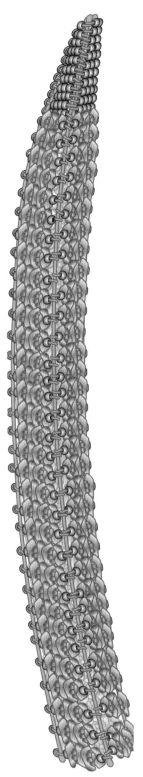

figure 6

Assemble

13 Cut a 10-inch (25.4 cm) piece of 16-gauge wire. Use the widest part of the round-nose pliers to make a large loop at one end. Insert the wire through the double-cone strap, slide the wire through the rest of the tube, and shape the strap into a gentle curve. At the other end, trim the wire ⅝ inch (1.6 cm) past the end of the cone. Use the widest part of the round-nose pliers to make a large loop.

14 Make 10 dangles. Each one consists of a size 11° seed bead and a keishi pearl strung on a head pin, with a wire wrapped loop at the top. Cut a second 10-inch (25.4-cm) piece of 16-gauge wire. Use the widest part of the round-nose pliers to make a large loop at one end. String all 10 dangles and the round lampworked bead onto the wire. Feed the wire through the wide end of the single-cone strap, pull taut, and shape the strap into a curve. Trim the wire ⅝ inch (1.6 cm) past the end of the cone. Use the widest part of the round-nose pliers to make a large loop.

15 Use chain-nose pliers to open the bottom loop of the double-end cone, attach it to the edge of the wheel component, and close the loop. Directly across from this connection, attach an open jump ring to the wheel, to the loop at the top of the elongated bead, and to the bottom loop of the single-end cone. Close the jump ring.

16 Follow the instructions on page 23 to create a wire hook clasp, using the same color size 11° seed beads as in the body of the necklace. Attach a single jump ring to the back of each strap, and catch the clasp in each jump ring.

SUPPLIES

Silver 20-gauge wire, 9 feet (2.8 m)

Silver 22-gauge wire, 18.5 feet (5.5 m)

Silver 26-gauge wire, 65 feet (20 m)

Size 15° seed beads:

Gold, 10 g

Purple metallic, 10 g

Green metallic, 10 g

37 olivine AB crystal bicones, 3 mm

50 jump rings, 18 gauge, 4.5 mm inner diameter

Basic Tool Kit, page 11

Steel mandrels:

0.05 inch (1.3 mm)

0.06 inch (1.6 mm)

FINISHED SIZE

19 inches (48.3 cm)

1 Cut 15 feet (4.6 m) of 22-gauge wire and make side-by-side wraps around the 0.05-inch (1.3 mm) steel mandrel to create a coil 18 inches (45.7 cm) long. Cut it into 46 segments, each ⅜ inch (1 cm) long.

CLEOPATRA NECKLACE

This necklace has a distinctly modern elegance. The bib shape captures the queen of the Nile's luxurious style, and triangles create the structure of the piece. They're also the building blocks of pyramids, and as such, they evoke the grandeur of a historical culture.

2 Coil 5 inches (12.7 cm) of 22-gauge wire around the 0.06-inch (1.6 mm) mandrel. Cut four short coils, each ⅜ inch (1 cm) long, from this long coil, and set them aside.

Create the Armatures

3 Cut 2 inches (5.1 cm) of 20-gauge wire. Mark each piece at the center and ⁹⁄₁₆ inch (1.4 cm) away from each side of the center mark. Repeat another 51 times, for a total of 52 pieces of marked wire.

4 Use chain-nose pliers to make to a 60° bend at the center mark on one of the pieces of wire. Then make a 45° bend at each of the other marks on it. All bends should be sharp, and the wire between the bends should be straight. Trim the ends to ¼ inch (6 mm). Slide a ⅜-inch (1 cm) coil onto the trimmed ends, and push the ends together inside of the coil (figure 1). Repeat 43 more times, for a total of 44 triangular armatures.

figure 1

5 Bend the remaining wires as described in step 4, and use them to create four diamond-shaped armatures. Each one is constructed by joining two triangles, as follows. Slide all four wire ends inside of one of the 1.6 mm diameter coils made in step 2. In the next section, the diamonds will be placed at each end of the geometric focal section of the necklace—triangles 1 and 2, and 51 and 52—and also used as triangles 23 and 24, and 29 and 30.

Weave the Triangles

When instructed to string, refer to figure 2 to determine which color of bead to use, depending on which triangle you are weaving.

figure 2

6 You'll begin by weaving the first triangle, labeled "1" on figure 2. Start by making a bead stop on one end of a 10-inch (25.4 cm) piece of 26-gauge wire. String 40 seed beads onto the wire. Anchor wrap the wire onto the triangle on one side of the point. This pattern will also be used for triangle 52.

7 Use a single-sided flat weave to add the seed beads to triangle 1.

Row 1: two beads
Row 2: four beads
Row 3: five beads
Row 4: six beads
Row 5: eight beads
Row 6: nine beads

After weaving each row in position, cross back to the opposite side of the triangle, leaving exposed wire behind the previous row of beads.

The next 50 triangles will be woven in single-sided flat weave using approximately 40 beads, with this count per row:

Row 1: one bead
Row 2: three beads
Row 3: four beads
Row 4: six beads
Row 5: seven beads
Row 6: eight beads
Row 7: nine beads

rows 1 and 2. Trim off the remaining wire, which will be used to attach the next triangle (figure 3).

figure 3

9 Wrap the wire twice around the next point, and attach the next two triangles together, working from the point toward the coil. Attach triangles into groups of four, following the diagram to keep track of the colors. Pay very close attention to the placement of the four diamond-shaped sections created earlier. Two diamonds are placed on each side of the center curve in the front, and the other two are placed at the back.

Embellish

10 Anchor wrap a 1-foot (30.5 cm) piece of 26-gauge wire around triangle 2, on the side with no other triangles attached. Pass the wire through the coil between triangles 1 and 2. Choose any one of the seed bead colors to use for this step, and string one seed bead, one bicone, and one seed bead, then go through the next coil. Continue around the outside "curve" of four triangles until a sequence of seed beads and a bicone is strung between all of the coils. After going through the fifth coil, wrap the wire twice and trim off the excess wire on both ends (figure 4).

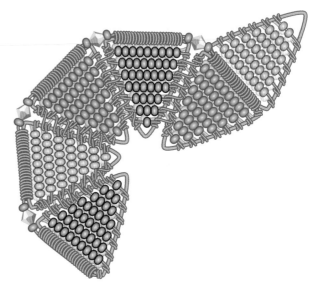

figure 4

Variation

After weaving each row in position, cross back to the opposite side of the triangle, leaving exposed wire behind the previous row of beads.

Attach the Triangles

8 Wrap a 1-foot (30.5 cm) piece of 26-gauge wire twice around the 20-gauge wire between rows 6 and 7. Cross over to the next triangle, go back underneath and come up between rows 5 and 6. Continue to wrap between each set of rows, working toward the point. Wrap twice between

11 Attach another 1-foot (30.5 cm) piece of 26-gauge wire next to the coil on triangle 7. Pass through the coil, string one seed bead, one bicone, and one seed bead between the coils, then continue the same pattern around the outside curve of triangles 7 through 10. After going through the coil on triangle 10, wrap the wire twice and trim off the excess wire on both ends (figure 5).

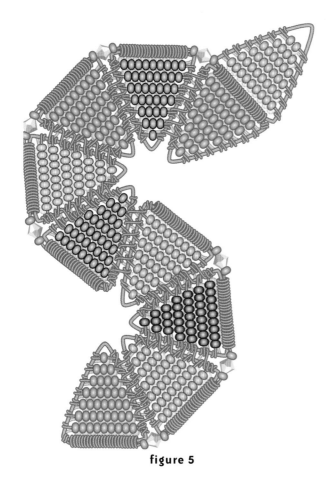

figure 5

12 Continue to attach seed beads and crystals through the rest of the outside curves. After you pass through the coil between triangles 51 and 52, wrap twice to end the wire.

13 Use two pairs of chain-nose pliers to attach a single jump ring through the point of triangle 1, and attach another jump ring to triangle 52.

Back

Finish

14 Assemble two sections of 1-in-1 jump-ring chain (page 23), each about 5 inches (12.7 cm) long. Attach one chain through the open row on triangle 1, and the other chain to triangle 52.

15 Make a wire hook clasp (starting on page 23) using any of the colors from the necklace for the wrapped beads in the middle of the clasp. Attach it to the loose end of one of the chains.

Note the dangle added to the 1-in-1 chain as an embellishment.

GALLERY

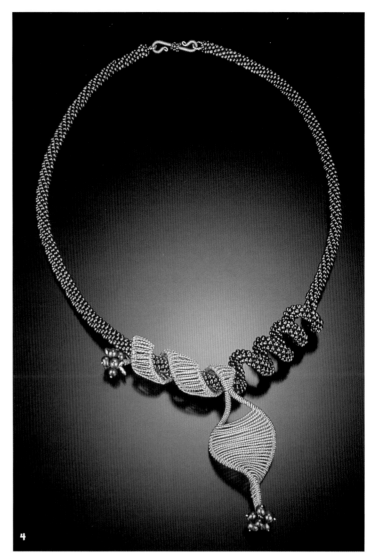

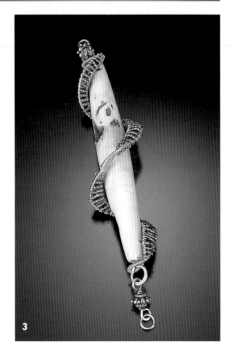

1 DALLAS LOVETT
Keishi Bracelet, 2002
19 x 1.3 cm
Keishi pearls, potato pearls, seed beads, silver wire; wire work
Photo by Robert Diamante

2 DALLAS LOVETT
Sand and Sable Bracelet, 2005
19.1 x 1.9 cm
Keishi pearls, seed beads, Bali silver, lampworked beads, silver wire; wire weaving
Photo by Robert Diamante

3 DALLAS LOVETT
Bead from *Galaxy Necklace,* 2005
8.9 x 1.9 cm
Tibetan bone bead, seed beads, silver wire; wire weaving
Photo by Robert Diamante

4 DALLAS LOVETT & LAUREL KUBBY
Autumn Leaf, 2002
Necklace, 68.5 cm long;
pendant, 12.7 x 3.8 cm
Potato pearls, seed beads, sterling silver wire; crochet, wire work
Photo by Robert Diamante

5 DALLAS LOVETT & LAUREL KUBBY
Ornate Treasures, 2002
11.4 x 6.4 cm
Seed beads, lampworked bead, silver wire; wire work
Photo by Robert Diamante

6 DALLAS LOVETT
Flight and Fantasy Necklace, 2005
45.7 x 17.8 cm
Seed beads, freshwater pearls, silver wire; wire weaving
Photo by Robert Diamante

7 DALLAS LOVETT
Art Nouveau, 2009
66.5 x 3.4 cm
Seed beads, Bali silver, sterling silver, Keishi pearls, crystal pearls; wire weaving
Photo by Robert Diamante

1 DALLAS LOVETT
Grecian Bracelet, 2004
8.9 x 1.9 cm
Seed beads, freshwater pearls, silver wire; wire weaving
Photo by Robert Diamante

2 DALLAS LOVETT
Boyer Wave, 2003
9.5 x 1.5 cm
Seed beads, dichroic glass, sterling silver; wire weaving, fabricated
using a cabachon and metal work
Photo by Robert Diamante

3 DALLAS LOVETT
Beaded Beads, 2005
Each, 6.5 x 8 cm
Seed beads, freshwater pearls, Bali silver, silver wire; wire weaving
Photo by Robert Diamante

4 DALLAS LOVETT & LAUREL KUBBY
Organic Desert, 2002
12.7 x 6.4 cm
Seed beads, keishi pearls, potato pearls, gold wire; herringbone stitch,
peyote stitch, wire work
Photo by Robert Diamante

5 DALLAS LOVETT
Ancient Moss, 2003
66 x 5 cm
Lampworked beads, seed beads, keishi pearls, sterling silver wire;
wire weaving, bead weaving
Photo by Robert Diamante

6 DALLAS LOVETT
Petite la Fleur, 2004
45.5 x 10 cm
Seed beads, freshwater pearls, keishi pearls, silver wire; wire weaving
Photo by Robert Diamante

7 DALLAS LOVETT
Galaxy Necklace, 2004
55.9. x 7.6 x 1.9 cm
Seed beads, freshwater pearls, lampworked beads, Bali silver, silver
wire; wire weaving
Photo by Robert Diamante

Photo by Roni Lovett

About the Author

In 1990, **Dallas Lovett** attended an Introduction to Beading class with his sister, Roni. Afterward he said, "Roni, let's open a bead store." Looking puzzled, she replied, "Okay, but where?" Within a year, their Tradewind Gallery was opened in a garage, and before long the pair were scheduling local and national artists to teach classes.

Dallas began teaching bead weaving, wirework, and polymer clay classes at the store. One day he strung seed beads on a sliver wire and was instantly fascinated. This began his weaving process with beads and wire. He loves the feel of wire and the texture of seed beads sliding through his hands. Making beautiful, elegant jewelry is his passion, and it has launched a career of teaching nationally and internationally.

Thanks to his bachelor's degree from the School of Fashion Design at Woodbury University in Los Angeles, California, Dallas is able to channel his design skills into wire art forms. Weaving supports—and defines—the structure of his jewelry; beads add texture and light. Placing the finished piece on the human body transforms it into dynamic, movable art.

Credits

Editors
Nathalie Mornu
Kevin Kopp

Technical Editor
Barb Switzer

Art Director
Kathleen Holmes

Illustrators
Melissa Grakowsky
J'aime Allene

Photographer
Stewart O'Shields

Art Intern
Lisa Maddox

Acknowledgments

Without the support and encouragement of the wire and beading community, this book would not be in your hands. I'm grateful to the people who have played a key role in my development as an artist and a teacher: Glenn Hixson, David Burman, and Marcia DeCoster. Each of them helped light my path on this journey.

One of the great inspirations of my life is the support of my family. My sister Roni is a fabulous photographer and maintains my website. Mom helped me daily to run the store and keep the books. She supported me every step of the way and is an incredible artist herself. Both of these strong women keep me grounded, give moral support, and share their wisdom. My father Jack has an awesome sense of humor and always told me to work hard and have fun. He provided the space for my studio to help me get started.

I want to thank Barb Switzer, a wonderful wire artist, my technical writer, and good friend. Barb took the time to listen to my concerns and numerous times she gave me back a bigger picture that allowed me to get unstuck and move ahead. Thank you to illustrator Melissa Grakowsky Shippee, too.

Many thanks to Joan Knutson, my studio assistant, for her guidance, friendship, and belief from day one that we could write a book that would be, as she said, "stunningly beautiful, with crystal clarity that would instantly inspire." Another essential part of the group was Rick Harris, a studio assistant with determination and razor-sharp writing skills.

Thanks to Nathalie Mornu and the people at Lark Crafts. Nathalie believed in me and has done everything possible to make the book-writing process go as smoothly as possible. I appreciated the clear communication of expectations that allowed us to work well together.

Finally, and most importantly, I thank my students from all over the world for standing by me. I have learned so much from you.

If I can do it, so can you.

Index

Awl 12, 21

Basic tool kit 11
Beads 9, 13
    Cabochon 8, 9, 20
    Crystals 9, 13
    Gemstones 9
    Pearls 9, 13
    Rivolis 9
    Seed 9, 13, 19, 20, 21, 24
Bead stop 17, 24
Bench block 11, 23
Bezel 8, 17, 20–22
Bracelets
    Braids 46
    Carré 42
    Circles 64
    Enchanted 60
    Infinity 49
    Rain Forest 56

Chain-nose pliers 11, 14, 15, 16, 23, 25
Chasing hammer 11, 23
Clasp 10
    see also Wire hook clasp
Coiling 16
Core wire 17, 18, 19, 20, 21, 22
Cuffs
    Arthurian 52
Culling 17
Cutters 10, 11, 14, 15, 18, 24

Drill 13, 16

Ear Wires 10, 11, 23
Earrings
    Crystal Magic 30
    High Rise 28
    La Fiesta 38
    Quasar 32

Files 12, 16, 26
Findings 10, 23
Fire bricks 12
Flush cutters 11, 15, 18, 22, 23, 24
Flux 10, 25, 26

Gallery 114–117
Gauge see Wire gauge

Hammering 12, 16, 23, 26
    see also Chasing hammer
    see also Mallet
Head pins 10, 12, 25
Hook 23, 24
Jump rings 10, 11, 16, 23
Jump-ring chain 23

Kinks 10, 11, 16, 17

Liver of sulfur 10, 26
Loops 14–15, 17

Mallet 11, 26
Micro torches 12, 25, 26
Mandrels 12, 13, 16, 26

Necklaces
    Cleopatra 110
    Diamonds 99
    Dreamscape 106
    Interchangeable 90
    Moroccan Jewels 96
    Nefertiti 92
    Wire-Go-Round 102
Nylon jaw pliers 11, 14

Oxidation 10, 17

Pendants
    Crown Jewel 76
    De Ros 81
    Entrapped Elegance 70
    Forbidden Fruit 78
    Phoenix Rising 84
    Saturn 72
Pickle 10, 12, 25, 26
Pliers see Chain-nose, Nylon jaw, or
    Round-nose
Polishing 13

Rings (findings) 10, 11, 16, 23
Rings (jewelry)
    The Ring 35
Rotary tumblers 13, 25, 26
Round-nose pliers 11, 14, 15, 17, 22, 23, 24

Soldering 12, 13, 25–26
Spacers 9
Spirals 15–16, 22
Steel bench block see Bench block
Steel shot 13

Tail see Wire tails
Tongs 12, 25, 26
Tweezers 12, 25, 26
Twisting 13, 16

Weaving
    Bezel 8, 20–22
    Dimensional tube 8
    Double-sided flat 8
    Single-sided flat 8
Weaving wire 17, 18, 19, 20, 21, 22
Wire 9, 10, 12, 13
Wire gauge (tool) 9, 10, 11, 13, 14, 17
Wire hook clasp 23
Wire tails 17
Work hardening 10, 16, 17

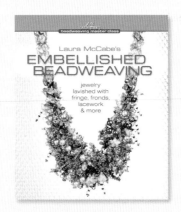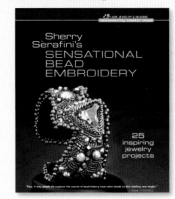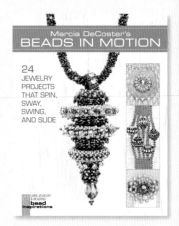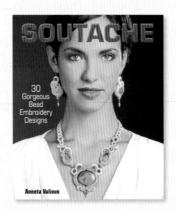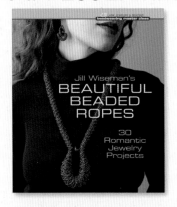